D0508311

Great Paragraphs

Great Paragraphs

An Introduction to Writing Paragraphs

Keith S. Folse
University of South Florida, Tampa

April Muchmore-Vokoun
University of South Florida, Tampa

Elena Vestri Solomon
University of South Florida, Tampa

Houghton Mifflin Company
Boston New York

Director of ESL Programs: Susan Maguire
Senior Associate Editor: Kathy Sands Boehmer
Developmental Editor: Kathleen M. Smith
Editorial Assistants: Lauren Wilson, Kevin M. Evans
Project Editor: Kellie Cardone
Senior Production/Design Coordinator: Jill Haber
Senior Manufacturing Coordinator: Priscilla Abreu

Cover Designer: Harold Burch Designs, NYC
Cover Image: Harold Burch Designs, NYC
Illustrations: Taz Sibley
Interior Design: Greta D. Sibley & Associates

Printed in the U.S.A.

Library of Congress Catalog Card Number: 98-72026

ISBN: 0-395-89155-8

123456789-CS-02 01 00

Contents

Part **II**   **Kinds of Paragraphs**   78

Overview

Great Paragraphs offers introductory material on paragraph writing. This material includes a wide variety of exercises that provide serious practice in both learning the writing process and developing a final written product. The book is designed for intermediate students; however, we have controlled the language as much as possible so that dedicated upper beginners and weak advanced students may also benefit from the instruction. Depending on the class level and the amount of writing that is done outside of class, there is enough material for 60 to 80 classroom hours. If a more substantial amount of writing is done outside of class, the number of hours for a faster group can be as little as 40.

The book contains 108 activities with approximately 50 suggestions for additional paragraph writing assignments. In addition, the appendices contain 30 supplementary practices in capitalization, punctuation, and grammar.

An important feature of *Great Paragraphs* is the inclusion of 95 sample paragraphs distributed throughout the activities. Instead of exercises consisting of unrelated sentences, the grammar practices present whole paragraphs of related sentences. In addition to providing relevant practice in the particular grammar point (or punctuation or capitalization area), these contextualized activities also provide learners with more input in English composition and paragraph organization and cohesion.

For many ESL students, not being able to write effectively and easily in English is a major obstacle to their future educational plans. Thus, the quality of any written work is important. To this end, the activities in this book deal with different elements that can affect the quality of a written product, including grammar, punctuation, and capitalization.

Some ESL students are already good writers in their native language, but others need work in the basic steps involved in the process of composing a paragraph. These students in particular will benefit from the step-by-step activities in *Great Paragraphs*.

The best judge of which units and which activities should be covered with any group of students is always the teacher. It is up to you to gauge the needs of your students and then match those needs with the material in this book.

TEXT ORGANIZATION

Great Paragraphs consists of three parts: Part 1 deals with the elements of a good paragraph, Part 2 features five different kinds of paragraphs, and Part 3 contains ancillary and additional practice material.

Part 1

Part 1 teaches, in general terms, how to construct a good paragraph. The five units in this first part cover 1) what a paragraph looks like, 2) how to brainstorm, 3) how to write a topic sentence, 4) what supporting and concluding sentences do, and 5) how to write a simple paragraph. Students who are already familiar with what a paragraph is may skip most of the material in Units 1 through 4, beginning instead with Unit 5, which reviews most of the material presented in Units 1 through 4. If students encounter problems, they could work on their problem areas by doing the pertinent activities in the earlier units. However, we believe students who have not done much work with paragraph writing should begin with Unit 1 and work through the book at a slower pace.

Part 2

Part 2 explains five different kinds of paragraphs: definition, process analysis, descriptive, opinion, and narrative. While it is not necessary to cover these five paragraph modes in this order, the current sequencing will allow for some recycling of grammatical and lexical items.

Part 3

Part 3 consists of six appendices. Appendix 1 explains the seven steps in the process of writing a paragraph. However, rather than merely listing the seven steps, as many books do, this appendix takes students through the process of the assignment in Unit 6, Definition Paragraphs. For the final assignment in this unit, a student has written a paragraph in which she defines an ethnic food, gumbo. Each of the seven steps is explained, followed by the student's writing in that step, whether it be brainstorming, handwritten notes about the process, or a rough draft.

Appendix 2 contains some general rules on capitalization in English. These are accompanied by several practice exercises. Appendix 3 follows a similar format for punctuation.

Many ESL students see grammar as their biggest problem. While other writing needs often deserve more attention, students recognize that their ability to express themselves in English is limited by the level of their English proficiency. To help with some of the most common grammar problems, Appendix 4 contains practice exercises.

Appendix 5 consists of peer editing sheets for the final writing activity in each unit. We believe that asking a student to comment on another student's paragraph without guidance is poor pedagogy and may result in hurt feelings for the writer. Not everyone is a good writer; therefore, we cannot assume that a less capable writer is able to make useful comments on a better writer's paper. Likewise, not all good writers know how to guide weaker writers toward an improved paragraph. These peer editing sheets provide focused guidance to help everyone make useful comments. For those students who are able to go beyond the basics, several of the questions are open-ended and invite additional comments.

Finally, Appendix 6 is the Answer Key.

CONTENTS OF A UNIT

Following are the common features of each unit. Though each unit has a specific writing goal and language focus (listed at the beginning of the unit), the following features appear in every unit.

Example Paragraphs

Because we believe that writing and reading are inextricably related, the example paragraphs are often preceded by short schema-building questions for small groups or the whole class. Potentially unfamiliar vocabulary is underlined in the paragraph and defined below. Example paragraphs are usually followed by questions about organization, syntactic structures, or other features.

Writer's Notes

Rather than large boxed areas overflowing with information, *Great Paragraphs* features small chunks of writing advice under this heading. The content of these notes varies from brainstorming techniques, to peer editing guidelines, to using adjectives to enliven writing.

Language Focus

This section directs students' attention to a grammar issue that is related to the kind of writing being practiced in that unit. Those students who need additional practice should work through any additional practices in Appendix 4.

Proofreading

Many of the units contain different kinds of proofreading exercises. We feel that a writer's ability to locate and repair problems in his or her own writing is a key skill for independent writing.

Sequencing

Even in the early units, students are asked to read sentences and put them in the best sequence. Where appropriate, students are asked to analyze the connecting or transition words and phrases. One of the main goals of *Great Paragraphs* is to teach writing devices, such as transition words, so that students will be better equipped to use them in their own writing. In addition, other activities focus on sequencing by asking the student to complete partial outlines of the material in a given paragraph.

Copying

In the early units, students are asked to sequence material or fill in the correct verb form. Students are then asked to copy these sentences in a paragraph format and add an original title. This exercise provides practice in what a paragraph looks like and the kinds of related information it contains. It also gets students writing early on.

Analyzing a Paragraph

Students are frequently asked to read a paragraph and answer a series of questions about various aspects of writing at the intermediate level, for example, recognizing the topic sentence, identifying the use of examples as support, or discovering the writer's purpose for including a given piece of information.

Original Writing

Each unit ends with at least one activity that requires students to do some form of original writing. In Part 1, students are often asked to write a paragraph of no specified rhetorical style. The purpose here is to practice developing a good paragraph from a solid topic sentence with good controlling ideas. In Part 2, students are expected to maintain the same standards while producing a different kind of paragraph in each unit. In addition, each of the units in Part 2 contains a list of five additional writing ideas or assignments. It is up to the teacher to decide whether all students will write about the same topic or whether each student is free to choose any of the five topics listed. In either case, we feel that better writing will result if students have the opportunity to discuss the topic of their writing in small groups as a pre-writing activity. Furthermore, it is our experience that having students discuss their ideas in groups of no more than five or six students results in maximum discussion in English, maximum exchange of ideas, and maximum participation from each individual.

Peer Editing

This is the last activity in each unit where students offer each other written comments with the goal of improving their paragraphs. Just as students have different writing abilities, so also do they have different editing abilities. For this reason, we believe that students benefit from guided peer editing. In Appendix 5 you will find a unique peer editing sheet for each unit. We recommend that students spend 15 to 20 minutes reading a classmate's paragraph and writing comments according to the questions on the peer editing sheet. Since a certain amount of trust and cooperation is involved in peer editing, it is important to make sure that students work with peers that they feel compatible with.

ABOUT THE ACTIVITIES AND PRACTICES

Teachers have long noticed that although students do well with grammar in discrete sentences, they may have problems with the same grammar when it occurs in a paragraph. Because of this, most of the activities and practices in *Great Paragraphs* work with complete paragraphs. Thus, instead of five unrelated sentences for practice with past tense, we offer a paragraph of five sentences. Our hope is that by practicing the grammatical problem in the target medium, students will produce more accurate writing sooner. The large number of such paragraphs (95) allows a great deal of freedom on the teacher's part in planning this course.

The earliest ESL composition textbooks were merely extensions of ESL grammar classes. The activities in these books did not practice English composition as much as they did ESL grammar points. Later books, on the other hand, tended to focus too much on the composing process. We feel that this focus ignores the important fact that the real goal for our ESL students is both to produce a presentable product and to understand the composing process. From our years of ESL and other L2 teaching experience, we believe that *Great Paragraphs* allows ESL students to achieve this goal.

ACKNOWLEDGMENTS

We would like to thank ESL and English composition colleagues who generously shared their ideas, insights, and feedback on L2 writing, university English course requirements, and textbook design. In addition, we would like to thank teachers on two electronic lists, TESL-L and TESLIE-L, who responded to our queries and thereby helped us write this book.

We would also like to thank our editors at Houghton Mifflin, Susan Maguire and Kathy Sands Boehmer, and our development editor, Kathleen Smith, for their indispensable guidance throughout the birth and growth of this project.

Likewise, we are indebted to the following reviewers who offered ideas and suggestions that shaped our revisions:

Sarah Mitchell Kim, Miramar College, CA

Virginia Scales, San Jose City College, CA

Colleen Weldele, Palomar College, CA

Kathy Flynn, Glendale Community College, CA

Rachel Gader, Georgetown University, Washington, DC

Jodi Brinkley, Florida Community College, FL

Chip DiMarco, Harvard University, MA

Janet Goldstein, Bramson ORT Technological Institute, NY

Kim Sanabria, Columbia University, NY

Tom Kitchens, Texas Intensive English Program, Austin, TX

Carol Thurston, North Virginia Community College, VA

Finally, many thanks go to our students who have taught us what ESL composition ought to be. Without them, this work would have been impossible.

Keith S. Folse

April Muchmore-Vokoun

Elena Vestri Solomon

Great Paragraphs

Part I

The Structure of a Paragraph

Unit 1

What Is a Paragraph?

GOAL: To learn the three main features of a paragraph

LANGUAGE FOCUS: Identifying verbs in sentences

What is a paragraph? One way to answer this question is to talk about words and sentences.

You know what a word is—a word represents an idea. It is composed of one or more letters. A word alone, however, is usually not enough to express thoughts. To communicate ideas, writers use sentences. A sentence is a collection of words that expresses a complete thought. A sentence usually consists of a subject and a verb.

The illustration below shows the relationship of the writing terms *letter*, *word*, *sentence*, *paragraph*, and *essay*. Letters can be combined into a word. Words can be combined into a sentence. Sentences can be combined into a paragraph. Finally, paragraphs can be combined into an essay. In this book, you will study paragraphs.

Connections

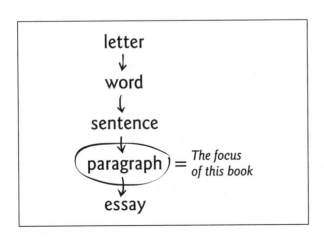

EXAMPLE PARAGRAPHS

Another way to learn about paragraphs is to read and study several examples. On the next few pages, you will find three paragraphs. Each is about a different topic and is written in a different style. Each shows what a good paragraph looks like and what a good paragraph sounds like.

Activity 1   **Studying an Example Paragraph**

Read and study this example paragraph. Then answer the questions that follow. The questions will help you understand the content of the paragraph.

Paragraph 1

This paragraph is about a method of written communication for people who cannot see. The underlined words are explained below.

Braille

Braille is a special system of writing and reading for <u>blind</u> people. Braille letters have groups of <u>bumps</u> or <u>dots</u>. Blind people read these dots by running their <u>fingertips</u> across them to recognize the <u>pattern</u> of the dots. Braille uses a special code of sixty-three characters. Each character has one to six dots that are <u>arranged</u> in a six-position pattern. For example, in the pattern for the letter C, the top two dots are <u>raised</u>, but the lower four are not. Braille gets its name from Louis Braille, a blind science and music teacher who <u>invented</u> this special alphabet in the 1800s. Millions of blind people are able to read today because of this simple yet effective communication system.

blind: not able to see	**pattern:** a design, a system
bump: a small, raised area	**arrange:** to put in a special way or order
dot: a small point	**raised:** higher than the surrounding area
fingertip: the end of the finger	**invent:** to create or make something original

1. In your own words, what is Braille? Begin your sentence: "Braille is . . ."

   _____

   _____

   _____

2. Have you ever seen Braille writing? If so, where?

   _____

_____

_____

3. Draw the Braille letters for a simple word. Then exchange books with a classmate to see if he or she can read your Braille word.

A	B	C	D	E	F	G	H	I	J
K	L	M	N	O	P	Q	R	S	T
U	V	X	y	Z	and	for	of	the	with
ch	gh	sh	th	wh	ed	er	ou	ow	W

_____

WRITER'S NOTE: Repetition and Present Tense

Two common features of paragraphs that explain or describe something are repetition and present tense verbs. "Braille," on page 4, explains and describes the Braille system.

Repetition

- How many sentences are there in the paragraph on the Braille system? _____

- Circle the subject of each sentence. (One sentence has two subjects.)

- How many times is *Braille* the subject of the sentence? _____

The word *Braille* is repeated because it is the topic that is being explained and described. Repetition of key nouns is sometimes necessary to avoid confusion.

Present Tense Verbs

- Put two lines under each verb in the paragraph on the Braille system. What

  tense are most of the verbs? _____

The correct answer is present tense. This paragraph explains something that we still use today, so most of the ideas are in the present tense.

- One verb is in the past tense. Write it here. _____

- Why do you think this verb is in the past tense? _____

Activity 2   Writing Practice

Think of something that is unique to your country or language or family. Write five sentences about that topic. What verb tense will you use?

1. _____

2. _____

3. _____

4. _____

5. _____

Activity 3   Studying an Example Paragraph

Read and study this example paragraph. Then answer the questions that follow. These questions will help you understand the content and the organization of the paragraph.

Paragraph 2

This paragraph tells how to do something. Read it and see if you can follow the steps.

An Easy Sandwich

An egg salad sandwich is one of the easiest and most delicious foods you can make. First, boil three eggs for five minutes. When the eggs are cool, peel away the shells and put the eggs into a bowl. Use a fork to mash them up very well. Add five tablespoons of mayonnaise. Add salt and pepper to taste. Mix these ingredients well. Allow the egg salad to cool in the refrigerator for thirty minutes. When you are ready to eat, spread the egg salad on bread and enjoy your creation.

EXAMPLE PARAGRAPH

boil: to cook in water at 212°F (100°C)

peel: to take away the outside cover of something

shell: the outside cover of an egg

mash: to push down and break into small pieces or mush

ingredients: the food items in a recipe

allow: to let

spread: to put all over something, like butter on bread

1. What is the main purpose of this paragraph? (Why did the author write this paragraph?)

_____

_____

_____

_____

2. Have you ever made egg salad? If so, is your recipe different? How?

_____

_____

_____

_____

3. Do you know an easier recipe? Write the main steps of the recipe and take turns presenting your information to the class.

_____

_____

_____

_____

_____

_____

WRITER'S NOTE: Imperative Form

Using the Imperative for Giving Directions

An English sentence that begins with a verb is called an imperative sentence. Imperative sentences are used to give directions or commands. The purpose of "An Easy Sandwich" on page 6 is to give directions, or steps, in completing a process—making egg salad. The writer uses imperative verb forms for most of the verbs in this paragraph.

Answer these questions:

- How many sentences are there in "An Easy Sandwich"? _____

- Circle the main verb in each sentence.

- How many sentences begin with a verb? _____

Sequence

When you give directions, the sequence is important—it should go from first to last. Read "An Easy Sandwich" again. Notice the sequence of the steps in making the recipe.

Activity 4   **Writing Practice**

Think of a process that you know how to do. Write four to seven sentences that explain how to do something.

1. _____

   _____

2. _____

   _____

3. _____

   _____

4. _____

   _____

5. _____

_____

6. _____

_____

7. _____

_____

| Activity 5 | Studying an Example Paragraph |

Read and study this example paragraph. Then answer the questions that follow. These questions will help you understand the content and the organization of the paragraph.

Paragraph 3

Can you remember a time when you had a strong feeling about something? Perhaps you were happy or sad or angry. In this paragraph, the writer tells about a day when he was afraid. This emotion was so strong that he remembers many details about the event even though it took place in 1972.

EXAMPLE PARAGRAPH

My First Flight

Although the first time I flew on a plane was many years ago, I can still remember how afraid I was that day. All my life I had wondered what it would be like to fly in an airplane. Finally, in March of 1972, I <u>boarded</u> my first flight. I flew from New Orleans to Managua, Nicaragua, on SAHSA Airlines. It was a Boeing 727 jet. There were three seats on each side of the <u>aisle</u>. It was <u>sort of</u> crowded, and this only made me more nervous. Every time we hit a little <u>turbulence</u>, my hands turned white. I was so nervous during the entire flight that I did not eat the meal they gave me. I would not even go to the bathroom. I cannot tell you how <u>relieved</u> I was when the plane finally landed at our <u>destination</u>. Since then, I have been on over one-hundred flights, but I can still remember even small details about my first airplane flight.

board: to get on a plane (or other form of transportation)

aisle: the row between seats on a plane (or bus or train)

sort of: somewhat, rather

turbulence: rough air during a flight, bumpiness

relieved: the feeling when there is no more pressure

destination: the final place you are traveling to

Write three questions for discussion about "My First Flight." Then work in small groups and take turns asking each other your questions. The first one has been done for you.

1. What do you remember about your first flight? _____

2. _____

    _____

3. _____

    _____

WRITER'S NOTE: Use of I and Past Tense

How is "My First Flight" different from "Braille" and "An Easy Sandwich"? "My First Flight" is a narrative paragraph. Writing that tells a story about something that happened is called narrative writing. Perhaps you already know the word "narrator." This is the person who tells the story.

Subjects

- How many sentences are there in this paragraph? _____

- Underline all the subjects.

- What word is used most often for the subject? _____

"My First Flight" is a narrative in which the narrator ("I") tells the events of his first trip on an airplane.

Past Tense Verbs

Most narrators tell a story about something that happened in the past. Most verbs in narrative writing are in the simple past tense.

- Underline all the verbs in "My First Flight."

- How many verbs are there? _____

- How many of the verbs are in the present tense? _____

- How many of the verbs are in the simple past tense? _____

You will learn more about narrative paragraphs in Unit 10.

Activity 6	**Writing Practice**

Think of something that happened to you. Write five to ten sentences in which you tell the story.

1. _____

2. _____

3. _____

4. _____

5. _____

6. _____

7. _____

8. _____

9. _____

10. _____

FOUR FEATURES OF A PARAGRAPH

These are the four main features of a paragraph:

1. **A paragraph has a topic sentence that states the main idea.** The topic sentence is the foundation for the paragraph. It can be at the beginning, in the middle, or at the end, but it is usually at the beginning. The topic sentence helps the reader understand what the paragraph is about. (Topic sentences will be discussed more in Unit 3.)

2. **All of the sentences in the paragraph are about one topic.** They are connected to the topic sentence. There are no unrelated or extra sentences. How do you know whether something is connected or not? Look at the ideas (also called controlling ideas) in the topic sentence. All other information in the paragraph must be connected to one or more of the controlling ideas in the topic sentence. (You will learn more about this on page 49.)

3. **The first line of a paragraph is indented.** This is easy to do. Just move the first line in about a half inch. On a typewriter or a word processor, this is about six spaces or the first tab stop position. This gap or open space in the first line is called an indentation.

4. **The last sentence, or concluding sentence, brings the paragraph to a logical conclusion.** For some writers, this is one of the most difficult features of a good paragraph. The concluding sentence usually states the main point again or summarizes the main idea of the paragraph. In addition, it can offer a prediction or a suggestion.

| Activity 7 | Analyzing the Features of a Paragraph |

Read this paragraph and answer the questions that follow.

Paragraph 4

EXAMPLE PARAGRAPH

Kids and Pets

At some point, most parents have to decide whether to allow their children to have pets. Some parents believe that pets teach children a sense of responsibility because children have to learn how to take care of their pets. In addition, many parents feel that pets can be fun for the family. Pets can also help children become more compassionate. On the other hand, some parents are afraid that their children might hurt the animals, or that these animals might hurt the children. Cats are good pets, but I don't like it when they shed hair on the furniture. Often these parents do not allow their children to have any kind of pet. Other families do not have the extra time or money that pets require. Although many children want a pet, parents are divided on this issue for a variety of important reasons.

1. What is the main idea of the paragraph?

_____

2. How many sentences are there in the paragraph? _____

3. How many sentences do not relate to the main idea? _____

4. Draw a line under the topic sentence. (Remember that the topic sentence is the sentence that helps the reader understand the main idea.)

5. How many lines (lines of text, not number of sentences) does this paragraph have? _____

6. What do you call the gap at the beginning of a paragraph? _____

7. Is this paragraph indented? _____

8. Draw two lines under the concluding sentence. How is the information in the concluding sentence related to the information in the topic sentence?

_____

_____

| Activity 8 | Analyzing the Features of the Example Paragraphs |

Look at the three example paragraphs again: "Braille" on page 4, "An Easy Sandwich" on page 6, and "My First Flight" on page 9. Complete the chart with information about the features of each paragraph.

Write the topic sentence.

"Braille" _____

"An Easy Sandwich" _____

"My First Flight" _____

What is the topic of the paragraph?

"Braille" _____

"An Easy Sandwich" _____

"My First Flight" _____

Is the first line indented?
    "Braille" ❏ yes ❏ no   "An Easy Sandwich" ❏ yes ❏ no   "My First Flight" ❏ yes ❏ no

| Activity 9 | Analyzing the Features of Student Paragraphs |

Read the following student paragraphs. Then answer the questions regarding the four main features of a paragraph. First, study this example.

Paragraph 5

Example

Computers Can Be a Student's Best Friend

Computers are excellent machines to help students. Before computers, students had to go to the library to do long, boring research. Many times students would read for four or five hours before finding something that was useful. These days, however, students can even use computers in their home to obtain the information that they need. Some computers are very expensive. My friend bought a computer that cost almost three thousand dollars. Computers have certainly made students' lives much easier.

1. Does the paragraph have a topic sentence? If so, write it here.

   Computers are excellent machines to help students.

2. What is the general topic of the paragraph?

   how computers help students

3. Are all the sentences related to the topic? If not, write the unrelated sentences here.

   Some computers are very expensive.

   My friend bought a computer that cost almost three thousand dollars.

4. Is the first line indented? __yes__

5. What is the concluding sentence?

   Computers have certainly made students' lives much easier.

Paragraph 6

EXAMPLE PARAGRAPH

William Henry Harrison

William Henry Harrison, the ninth president of the United States, is famous for several things. He was the only president who studied to become a doctor although he did not finish medical school. On March 4, 1841, he made the longest inaugural speech by any president. A few days later, he caught a cold that developed into pneumonia. On April 4, 1841, he became the first president who died in office after serving the shortest term of any president—less than a month. His widow was also the first First Lady to receive a pension—$25,000. It is ironic that William Henry Harrison, who was president for such a short time, is better known than many of the presidents who served full terms.

1. Does the paragraph have a topic sentence? If so, write it here.

   _____

2. What is the topic of the paragraph?

   _____

3. Are all the sentences related to the topic? If not, write the unrelated sentences here.

   _____

   _____

   _____

4. Is the first line indented? _____

5. Underline the concluding sentence.

Paragraph 7

EXAMPLE PARAGRAPH

The State of South Carolina

First, South Carolina is an important manufacturing and farming state. One of its most important crops is tobacco. The second reason involves American history. Many important battles of the American Revolution took place in South Carolina. In addition, on December 20, 1860, South Carolina became the first state to leave the United States. Four months later, the Civil War between the North and the South began in Charleston, a seaport in this state.

← South Carolina

1. Does the paragraph have a topic sentence? If so, write it here.

   _____

2. What is the topic of the paragraph?

   _____

3. Are all the sentences related to the topic? If not, write the unrelated sentences here.

   _____

   _____

   _____

4. Is the first line indented? _____

Paragraph 8

EXAMPLE PARAGRAPH

Jim Thorpe's Final Victory

Jim Thorpe won Olympic gold medals in 1912, but he wasn't allowed to keep them. In the 1912 Games, Thorpe won both the pentathlon (five events) and decathlon (ten events). However, a month later, the U.S. Olympic Committee took away his medals because Thorpe had played baseball for money. An athlete who takes money for sports is called a professional, and at that time, professional athletes were not allowed to take part in any Olympic Games. In 1982, the U.S. Olympic Committee reversed this ruling. Seventy years after his achievements, Thorpe's name was finally returned to the list of 1912 Olympic winners.

1. Does the paragraph have a topic sentence? If so, write it here.

   _____

2. What is the topic of the paragraph?

   _____

3. Are all the sentences related to the topic? If not, write the unrelated sentences here.

   _____

   _____

   _____

4. Is the first line indented? _____

5. What time phrases in the concluding sentence make the sentence sound like the ending of the

   paragraph? _____ , _____

Paragraph 9

EXAMPLE PARAGRAPH

Skipping Breakfast

Statistics show that many Americans skip breakfast, and the reasons for this do not surprise me because I am a member of this group. I am not a "morning person," so it is extremely hard for me to wake up and then prepare breakfast. In addition, I don't like to eat breakfast because it makes me feel full all morning. With this uncomfortable feeling in my stomach, it is difficult for me to do my work well. Finally, I am very concerned about my health, so I avoid the fatty kinds of breakfast foods that Americans traditionally eat such as scrambled eggs, buttered toast, or fried sausage. Although others may not agree with my decision, I prefer to skip breakfast.

1. Does the paragraph have a topic sentence? If so, write it here.

   _____

2. What is the topic of the paragraph? _____

   _____

3. Are all the sentences related to the topic? If not, write the unrelated sentences here.

_____

_____

_____

4. Is the first line indented? _____

5. Read the concluding sentence again. Do you think the author might change his opinion about skipping breakfast? Why?

_____

Paragraph 10

EXAMPLE PARAGRAPH

My First Class

I can still remember the first day I taught a class. I was twenty-three years old. I had just graduated from college. The six weeks of practice teaching that I had done was very different from teaching my own class. When I walked into the room, I was extremely nervous. I carefully put my books down on the desk. Then I heard a girl say something in Spanish to another classmate. She told her friend to look at my hands because they were trembling so much. I was wearing a new watch that day, too. She did not know that I could understand Spanish. I smiled and she started to laugh because she realized that I understood Spanish. After all these years, I can still remember this small incident and how it helped me relax on my first day of teaching.

1. Does the paragraph have a topic sentence? If so, write it here.

_____

2. What is the topic of the paragraph?

_____

3. Are all the sentences related to the topic? If not, write the unrelated sentences here.

_____

_____

_____

4. Is the first line indented? _____

5. Sometimes key words or phrases appear in both the topic sentence and the concluding sentence.

   What words are repeated in both the topic sentence and the concluding sentence?

   _____

Activity 10	**Capitalization and End Punctuation**

Write each sentence with correct capitalization and end punctuation. See Appendix 2 and Appendix 3, pages 169–179, if you need help.

Example: each year thousands of people move to florida

Each year thousands of people move to Florida.

1. this increase in the number of residents means more money for the state

   _____

   _____

2. more public funding will result in better facilities and services for the state's current residents

   _____

   _____

3. however, is this increase in population really such a good thing for the state

   _____

   _____

4. some people see problems

   _____

   _____

5. these floridians are concerned that the state is not able to handle more people

_____

_____

6. some conservationists worry about environmental damage in the everglades

_____

_____

7. others worry about the decreasing supply of fresh drinking water

_____

_____

8. thus, the increase in new residents and money may not be a positive thing

_____

_____

WORKING WITH PARAGRAPHS

In this section, you will begin to get the feel of a paragraph by copying sentences into paragraphs and writing one of your own.

Activity 11   **Copying a Paragraph**

Copy the sentences from Activity 10 in the same order. Make sure your paragraph is indented. Write a title on the top line.

Paragraph 11

_____

_____

_____

_____

_____

_____

_____

_____

_____

_____

LANGUAGE FOCUS: Identifying Verbs in Sentences

Every sentence in English has a verb. Look at the verbs in these examples.

1. Where <u>is</u> the bank?
2. Japan <u>produces</u> many different kinds of cars.
3. Wheat <u>is grown</u> in Argentina.
4. The house on the corner <u>doesn't have</u> a garage.
5. Mr. Peters <u>speaks</u> French and Italian.

Read the same five sentences without the verbs. A sentence without a verb is called a fragment. The word *fragment* means a piece of something that has been broken off. You will study more details about fragments in the Language Focus on page 45.

1. Where the bank?
2. Japan many different kinds of cars.
3. Wheat in Argentina.
4. The house on the corner not a garage.
5. Mr. Peters French and Italian.

WRITER'S NOTE: Check for the Verb

Though you do not need to worry about every grammar mistake in your writing, one very serious mistake is forgetting the verb.

Remember: Every sentence in English must have a verb. Before you turn in your paper in any class, you should proofread it. Some mistakes are difficult to catch, but a sentence without a verb is easy to spot. Always check each sentence to make sure there is a verb!

| Activity 12 | Checking Your Grammar |

Read each sentence. The subject in each clause is in italics. Underline the verb that goes with each subject. If every subject in the sentence has a verb, write C for "correct" on the line. If a subject does not have a verb, write X on the line and add an appropriate verb in the correct place. (Many different verbs can be used. Use any one that you think is appropriate.) The first one has been done for you.

                                                                         exist

1. __X__ We know that *languages* <u>vary</u>, but other important communication *methods* ∧ .

2. _____ For example, when two *people* are talking, the appropriate *amount* of space between them varies by culture.

3. _____ In some cultures, *people* near each other when having a conversation.

4. _____ Sometimes these *people* might touch each other during the conversation.

5. _____ *Not standing near the speaker or not touching* might be seen as "cold" or disinterested behavior.

6. _____ In other cultures, *people* stand farther apart.

7. _____ If *one* of the speakers too close, the other *person* might see this as aggressive or strange behavior.

8. _____ The *amount* of personal space from culture to culture.

9. _____ *It* also a form of communication.

10. _____ Just as there is no universal *language*, there is no universal personal *space*.

| Activity 13 | Copying a Paragraph |

Copy the sentences from Activity 12 in the same order. Make sure your paragraph is indented. On the top line, write an original title for your paragraph.

Paragraph 12

_____

_____

_____

_____

_____

_____

_____

_____

_____

_____

_____

_____

| Activity 14 | Original Writing Practice |

Now it is your turn to write a simple paragraph. Follow these guidelines:

- Choose a general topic.

- Think of some specific aspect of that topic. Try to be as specific as you can. For example, you might choose "sports" as your first idea. Then you might choose "tennis." Finally, you might choose "How to Keep Score in Tennis."

- Write five to twelve sentences.

- Include a topic sentence.

- Indent the first line.

- Give your paragraph a title.

You can choose any topic you want. The topics and topic sentences below may help you with ideas. In future units, you will learn how to get ideas and develop them into paragraphs.

Topic	Topic Sentence
Food	The easiest food to prepare is . . .
	The best meal I ever had was . . .
Color	Each color in my country's flag represents something special.
	Colors can affect the way you feel.
Sports	My favorite football (or other sport) player is . . .
	The rules for _____ (name a sport) are not so (easy / difficult).
People	My favorite person in the world is . . .
	If I could meet anyone in history, I would like to meet . . .

INTRODUCTION TO PEER EDITING

Many students think that writing a paragraph only once is enough. This is rarely true. Even skilled and professional writers write and edit more than one draft.

WRITER'S NOTE: Once Is Not Enough!

Think of the first draft of your paper as your first attempt. Before you rewrite, it is helpful to let someone read your paper, offer comments, and ask questions about your meaning. Many writers do not always see their own mistakes, but a reader can help you see where you need to make improvements.

Sometimes you need more than one opinion about your paper. In class, peer editing is an easy way to get opinions about your paper. In this method, other students (your peers) read your paper and make comments using a set of questions and guidelines (in Appendix 5). You will read someone else's paper, too. Peer editing can help you clear up any areas that are not strong or that appear confusing to the reader.

WRITER'S NOTE: Suggestions for Peer Editing

Listen Carefully

In peer editing, you will receive many comments and some suggestions from other students. It is important to listen carefully to comments about your writing. You may think that what you wrote is clear and accurate, but readers can often point out places that need improvement. Remember that the comments are about the writing, not about you!

Make Helpful Comments

When you read your classmates' papers, choose your words and comments carefully so that you don't hurt their feelings. For example, instead of saying "This is bad grammar" or "I can't understand any of your ideas," make helpful comments, such as "You need to make sure that every sentence has a verb" or "What do you mean in this sentence?"

Activity 15	Peer Editing

In this activity, you will exchange papers with a peer and read each other's papers. Your main purpose is to help your classmate with ways to improve his or her paragraph. It is equally valuable for you to read other people's writing so you can see different ways of organizing ideas.

Choose someone that you work well with. Exchange paragraphs from Activity 14. Then use Peer Editing Sheet 1 on page 191 to help you comment on your partner's paper. It is important to offer positive comments that will help the writer.

Unit 2

Developing Ideas for Writing a Paragraph

GOAL: To learn how to brainstorm ideas for writing

LANGUAGE FOCUS: Identifying verbs in sentences (reinforcement)

Imagine that you are in a room on the fourth floor of a hotel when suddenly the fire alarm goes off. You cannot go out the door of your room because the hallway is filled with smoke. The window looks like the only exit, but you are on the fourth floor. What will you do?

Make a list of at least three ideas. Work quickly. Do not worry about how good the idea is or about correct writing. The goal is to create a list as quickly as possible.

1. _____

_____

2. _____

_____

3. _____

_____

Congratulations! You have just finished your first *brainstorming session*. Now compare your list with other students' lists.

BRAINSTORMING

Brainstorming is quickly writing down all the thoughts that come into your head. When you brainstorm, you do not think about whether the idea is good or bad or whether your writing is correct. You simply write to get your ideas on paper. This process is called brainstorming because it feels like there's a storm in your brain—a storm of ideas!

Brainstorm your ideas!

Activity 1   **Brainstorming Practice**

Use this topic and situation to practice brainstorming.

Next Saturday is your grandmother's birthday. She is going to be eighty-eight years old. What will you get for her? Make a list of five suitable birthday gifts for a person this age.

1. _____

2. _____

3. _____

4. _____

5. _____

Compare your list to a classmate's list. Did you get more gift ideas from your classmate? Sometimes it is helpful to work with other writers and share ideas. Remember that in brainstorming, there are no bad ideas. The purpose of brainstorming is to produce as many ideas as possible and not worry about correct grammar and punctuation.

WRITER'S NOTE: The Importance of Brainstorming

Brainstorming is like a storm of ideas in your brain. A good writer thinks about the topic first and writes words and ideas—brainstorms about the topic. It is important to remember that the first step in writing a paragraph is not writing—it is thinking.

On the next page is an example of brainstorming for Paragraph 2, "An Easy Sandwich," on page 6. This is the original brainstorming, so there are several ideas that were not included in the final paragraph. In addition, there are a few ideas in the final paragraph that are not in this list.

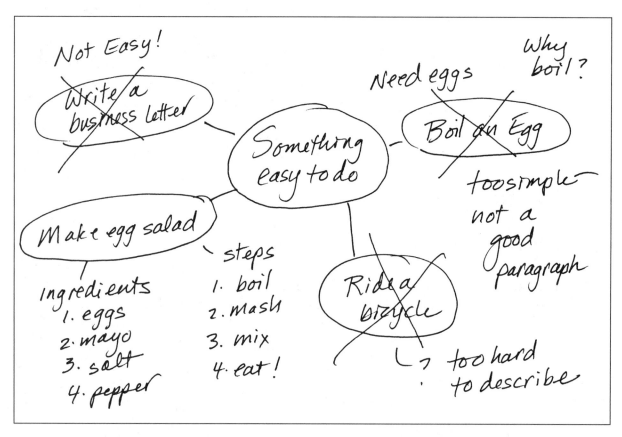

The writer brainstormed four different ideas for the assignment. Can you tell which one was chosen? Would you have made the same choice?

HOW BRAINSTORMING WORKS

From the diagram, you can see that the writer wrote many ideas and crossed out some of them. Brainstorming is not a linear or a consecutive process. Instead, it can be a messy process. Writers move from one idea to another, then back to an earlier idea, then forward again to a new idea, and so on. They cross out words, draw lines to make connections, and change their minds.

Brainstorming involves associating ideas—one idea produces another. Some writers brainstorm in lists. Others cluster or connect their ideas in some way. Brainstorming can help writers visualize the paragraph.

Activity 2 — Brainstorming Practice

Follow these steps for each of the example topics:

1. Read the topic.
2. Brainstorm about the topic in the box. Write a list or use the diagram on page 28 as an example of how to connect ideas.
3. Circle the ideas that you think are best to include in a paragraph.
4. Compare and discuss your ideas with your partner. When you compare your notes, be prepared to say why you want to keep some ideas and why you want to take out others. What information will be in the final paragraph?

Topic A: How the weather affects people

Brainstorm area:

Topic B: the value of space exploration

Brainstorm area:

| Activity 3 | **Brainstorming Practice from Example Paragraphs** |

Choose an example paragraph that you read in Unit 1: "Braille," "An Easy Sandwich," or "My First Flight." Brainstorm ideas for a paragraph that is related to the topic of one of these paragraphs.

- Which paragraph did you choose? _____

- Why did you choose this paragraph? _____

_____

Use the space below to brainstorm. If you want, work with another student who chose the same topic. Sometimes when you work with another writer, you get more ideas.

Brainstorm area:

LANGUAGE FOCUS: Subject-Verb Agreement

All sentences in English contain a verb. The regular present tense has two forms: the base form and the *-s /-ies* form. For example, here are the two forms of the verb *prepare.*

prepare   I prepare. They prepare.

prepares   He prepares.

The *-s* form is used for third person singular (*he, she, it*).

Common Mistakes

- One of the most common mistakes for nonnative writers is to omit the *-s /-ies* in the present tense. Another common mistake is to write *-s /-ies* when the verb is not third person singular. This is an error in subject-verb agreement. The form of the verb depends on the subject of the sentence. If you first find the subject, then you can write the verb correctly.

- Another common subject-verb agreement mistake involves prepositional phrases. A prepositional phrase includes a preposition (for example, *for, at, from, by, with, without, in, of*) and the noun or pronoun that follows.

Example: The owner <u>of these restaurants</u> is Italian.
(PREPOSITION: *of;* NOUN: *restaurants*)

The noun in a prepositional phrase does not affect the number (singular or plural) of the verb in the sentence. Some students choose the form of the verb by looking at the nearest noun. Remember that the noun in a prepositional phrase is NEVER the subject of a sentence.

Study the following examples. In each sentence, the subject is underlined once, the verb is in bold type, and the prepositional phrase is italicized. Notice that the verb agrees with the subject, even when the noun in the prepositional phrase comes between the subject and the verb.

The main <u>product</u> *of Brazil* **is** coffee.

The main <u>product</u> *of Brazil and Colombia* **is** coffee.

The main <u>products</u> *of Brazil* **are** coffee and aluminum.

Here are four sentences that nonnative students wrote. Can you identify the mistakes and correct them?

1. In my country, most people lives near the coast because the interior is too dry.

2. A pair of scissors are necessary for this project.

3. Joseph carry his guitar from class to class every Thursday.

4. The main method of transportation in all of those tropical islands are the public bus system.

Activity 4	Subject–Verb Agreement Practice

Read this student paragraph. It contains several subject-verb errors. Underline the errors and write the correct form above them.

Paragraph 13

Teaching Is Hard Work!

EXAMPLE PARAGRAPH

Charlotte Jenkins is a kindergarten teacher at King Elementary School. Every day she leaves home at 7:20 A.M. She lives near the school, so she walk to school when the weather is nice. She usually arrive just before 8:00, and the kindergarten students in her class arrives between 8:10 and 8:30. Mrs. Jenkins' class begin at 8:30, but she does a lot before class begins. She has to make sure the room is ready for her students. She have to

EXAMPLE PARAGRAPH

make sure that the teacher's aide knows the lesson plan. She teaches from 8:30 to noon.

This year she has twenty-two students. She says that these young children keeps her

extremely busy. She loves her job, but it is a lot of hard work. She says that people does

not realize how hard this kind of job is. She has been teaching kindergarten for eleven

years. She hopes to continue teaching for many more years.

Activity 5	Writing a Paragraph from Brainstorming

Choose a topic from Activity 2 on pages 29–30. Use the ideas that you brainstormed about that topic to write a paragraph. Include the four features of a paragraph on pages 11–12.

Activity 6	Peer Editing

Exchange your paragraph from Activity 4 with a partner's paragraph. Use Peer Editing Sheet 2 on page 193 to help you comment on your partner's paper. It is important to offer positive comments that will help the writer.

Unit 3

The Topic Sentence

GOAL: To learn how to write a topic sentence

LANGUAGE FOCUS: Sentence fragments and comma splices

In Unit 1 you learned that a good paragraph has these four features:

1. A paragraph has a topic sentence that states the main idea.

2. All of the sentences in the paragraph are about one topic.

3. The first line of a paragraph is indented.

4. The concluding sentence brings the paragraph to a logical ending.

In this unit, you will learn the answers to these questions about the topic sentence:

- What does a topic sentence do?

- What does a good topic sentence look like?

- How can you tell if a sentence would be a good topic sentence?

- Where is a topic sentence usually found in a paragraph?

Activity I	Recognizing Effective Topic Sentences

What do you already know about topic sentences? Read the sentences in each number and decide which one would be the best topic sentence. Put a check (✔) on the line. Be prepared to explain your answers.

1. _____ Winter is a good season.

   _____ Winter weather is cold, and it snows.

   _____ The best season for kids is winter.

2. _____ Soccer is the world's most popular sport.

   _____ You need a leather ball to play soccer.

   _____ Soccer is a nice game.

3. _____ There are many people in Los Angeles.

   _____ People from many different cultures live in Los Angeles.

   _____ Los Angeles is a big city in California.

4. _____ Monolingual dictionaries have only one language, and bilingual

   dictionaries have two languages.

   _____ Many language students prefer bilingual dictionaries to monolingual dictionaries.

   _____ Dictionaries that have two languages, such as French and English, are called bilingual

   dictionaries.

5. _____ French perfumes are expensive for a number of reasons.

   _____ My mother's perfume smells flowery.

   _____ You can purchase perfumes in expensive blue crystal bottles.

6. _____ *An American Tragedy* has 946 pages.

_____ A woman drowns in *An American Tragedy*.

_____ *An American Tragedy* is an excellent psychological novel.

How did you decide which sentences would be the best topic sentences? What were you looking for?

FEATURES OF A GOOD TOPIC SENTENCE

A good topic sentence has the following features:

- It controls or guides the whole paragraph. When you read the topic sentence, you know what to expect in the paragraph.

- A good topic sentence is not a general fact that everyone accepts as true. *Libraries have books* is not a good topic sentence.

- A good topic sentence is specific. *Tea is delicious* is not a good topic sentence because it is too general. The reader does not know what to expect in the paragraph. *Green tea has many health benefits* is a good topic sentence because it is specific.

- A good topic sentence is not too specific. *This monolingual dictionary contains more than 42,000 words* limits the topic too much—there is nothing else for the writer to say.

- A good topic sentence often has controlling ideas—words or phrases that help guide the flow of ideas in the paragraph.

Controlling Ideas

Here are some example topic sentences with controlling ideas. The controlling ideas have been underlined.

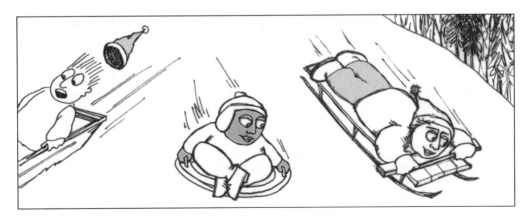

1. The <u>best season</u> for <u>kids</u> is winter.

   Explanation: *Best season* and *kids* are the controlling ideas. The reader expects the paragraph to give reasons and examples why winter is the best season for children.

2. Soccer is the <u>world's most popular sport</u>.

   Explanation: *World's most popular sport* is the controlling idea. The reader expects
   the paragraph to give a variety of information about soccer and why
   it is popular around the world.

3. People from <u>many different cultures</u> live in Los Angeles.

   Explanation: *Many different cultures* is the controlling idea. The reader expects
   the paragraph to include information about various groups of people
   who make up the population of Los Angeles.

4. Many <u>language students</u> <u>prefer bilingual</u> dictionaries <u>to monolingual</u> dictionaries.

   Explanation: *Language students* and *prefer bilingual to monolingual* are the controlling ideas. The reader expects the paragraph to explain why this
   statement is true.

| Activity 2 | **Recognizing Controlling Ideas in Topic Sentences** |

Read the topic sentences and underline the controlling ideas. Then explain what
information you expect to find in the paragraph.

1. The SAT contains two distinct sections that deal with two different skills.
   Explanation:

   _____

   _____

2. The shocking crash of a 747 jumbo jet off the coast of New York has baffled investigators.
   Explanation:

   _____

   _____

3. Though buying a house may seem appealing, renting an apartment has many advantages.
   Explanation:

   _____

   _____

4. Recent research has confirmed that eating dark green, leafy vegetables such as broccoli and cabbage may reduce the risk of some types of cancer.

Explanation:

_____

_____

5. Crossword puzzles are not only educational and fun but also addictive.
Explanation:

_____

_____

Activity 3	More Practice Recognizing Controlling Ideas

Read the sentences in each number. Put a check (✓) next to the best topic sentence. Underline the controlling ideas in that sentence. Be prepared to explain your answers.

1. _____ Most of the girls in the class get higher grades in Spanish than the boys.

   _____ Research has shown that girls are better at languages than boys.

   _____ Many students like languages very much.

2. _____ Cats are better pets than dogs for many reasons.

   _____ Cats and dogs are both mammals.

   _____ Cats can't swim very well, but dogs can.

3. _____ Yesterday I didn't have lunch with my co-workers.

   _____ Yesterday I went to work late.

   _____ Yesterday was the worst day of my life.

4. _____ Some people call George Washington the Father of Our Country.

   _____ Because of his numerous contributions to the United States, George Washington is often

   called the Father of Our Country.

   _____ George Washington became president of the United States in 1789, and he is often called

   the Father of Our Country.

5. _____ Many Canadians speak French, and some of them speak Chinese and Japanese.

   _____ The current population of Canada is a reflection of the international background of

   its citizens and immigrants.

   _____ A large number of new immigrants live in the western province of British Columbia,

   but not many of them speak German.

Activity 4	More Practice with Controlling Ideas

All of these topic sentences are too general. Write each sentence again with controlling ideas.
Compare your sentences with other students' sentences.

Example: Flowers are beautiful.

   Flowers are the best gift to receive when you are feeling down.
   _____

                                    or

   Only four kinds of flowers grow during the short summers in Alaska.
   _____

1. Cats are nice.

   _____

2. Paris is the capital of France.

   _____

3. The English alphabet has twenty-six letters.

   _____

   _____

4. It costs forty cents to mail a first-class letter from the United States to Canada.

   _____

   _____

5. Tennis is an enjoyable sport.

   _____

WORKING WITH TOPIC SENTENCES

Now it's time to write some topic sentences.

| Activity 5 | **Writing Topic Sentences** |

Read each paragraph and write a good topic sentence for it. Be sure to end each topic sentence with correct punctuation.

Paragraph 14

1. _____

   _____

EXAMPLE PARAGRAPH

Young people tend to buy them because they want to look "cool" to their friends. It's much easier to get a date if you drive a Corvette Stingray than if you borrow your father's station wagon. Wealthy people, however, enjoy sports cars because they want to show others that they have "status" in their community. I've never seen a doctor or a lawyer driving around in an old Volkswagen. Finally, sports cars appeal to adventurers. These are people who like to take risks on the road. Whatever the reasons, I think sports cars are here to stay!

Paragraph 15

2. _____

_____

One is size. Dinosaurs were much, much larger than any animal we have on Earth today. Second, the legs of most reptiles today are on the sides of their body. Dinosaurs' legs, however, were on the bottom of their body. In this way, dinosaurs could stand up on their back legs.

Paragraph 16

3. _____

_____

First, your body will look better. Exercise is perfect for staying trim and healthy-looking, and it's more fun than dieting. Second, you will actually have more energy. A person who exercises will have fewer problems walking up stairs or climbing hills. In addition, your heart will be healthier. A good, strong heart is necessary for a long, healthy life. Finally, exercise reduces stress and keeps your mind in shape. So, if you want to improve your overall health, exercise is an excellent method.

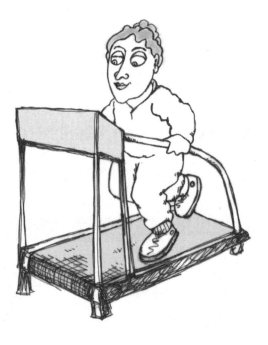

Paragraph 17

4. _____

_____

It is without doubt one of the easiest foods to eat. You don't need any special utensils. It doesn't have to be served piping hot like some foods do. In addition, with only 20 calories per cup and almost no fat, it is both a filling and a heart-friendly snack. Furthermore, it can be an important source of natural fiber, a substance that has been shown to be important in limiting certain types of cancer. Based on this information, can anyone be surprised that sales of popcorn are soaring all across the country?

Paragraph 18

(This one is more difficult than the others. Good luck!)

5. _____

_____

EXAMPLE PARAGRAPH

In this method, learners form their own sound association between the foreign language word they are trying to learn and any word in their native language. In the second stage, learners form an image link between the target word and the native language word. For example, a Japanese learner of English might look at the English word *hatchet* and connect it to the Japanese word *hachi,* which means "eight." In his head, the learner might remember that he can use a hatchet eight times to cut down a tree. An English speaker learning Spanish might remember the word *trigo* (wheat) by using the English words *tree* and *go.* For some people, this particular method is effective.

WRITER'S NOTE: Keep a Journal for New Ideas

If you don't have a good topic for your paragraph, then it's hard to write a solid, interesting topic sentence. Many students say, "I don't know what to write about." A good source for ideas is a personal journal. A journal is a notebook in which you write ideas about any topic you want. If you don't know what to write, then just write what you did today or how you're feeling about an experience. Later you can read your journal again; you may be surprised to find many good ideas for topics.

Activity 6   **Comma Practice**

Insert commas in these sentences where necessary. Be prepared to explain your choices. See Appendix 3, page 174, if you need help. Some sentences may be correct.

1. Malaysia and Thailand are two countries in Southeast Asia.

2. Because they are located next to each other, we might expect these two

   nations to share many similarities.

3. To a certain extent this is true.

4. Both countries have temperate climates throughout the year.

5. Thailand's economy is growing and so is Malaysia's.

6. Malaysia has miles of beautiful beaches that attract tourists and Thailand does, too.

7. However there are many differences as well.

8. Malaysians and Thais speak completely different languages.

9. Most Malaysians are Muslim and most Thais are Buddhist.

10. Thailand has a national king but Malaysia does not.

11. Malaysia was a British colony but Thailand was never a British colony.

12. Thus the fact that two countries are near each other does not always mean

    they are similar.

Activity 7	**Copying a Paragraph**

Copy the sentences from Activity 6 in the same order. Make sure your paragraph is indented. On the top line, write an original title for your paragraph.

Paragraph 19

_____

_____

_____

_____

_____

_____

_____

_____

_____

_____

LANGUAGE FOCUS: Sentence Fragments and Comma Splices

Two common mistakes in writing are sentence fragments and comma splices. These mistakes can prevent the reader from understanding the writer's message, so they are serious errors.

Sentence Fragments

A sentence fragment is not a complete sentence. It is usually missing either a subject or a verb. A sentence fragment does not make sense by itself. It is just a piece of the whole idea. The easiest way to correct a fragment is to add the missing part. The missing part is usually a subject or a verb.

Read these sentence fragments that nonnative speakers wrote. The fragments are underlined.

1. Last summer I went to Italy. <u>Was a wonderful trip</u>. I want to go again if I can.

   Correction: **It** was a wonderful trip. (Add a subject.)

2. George Washington was president for eight years. Many people wanted him to continue as president, but he refused. <u>A very difficult decision for Washington</u>.

   Correction: **This was** a very difficult decision for Washington. (Add a subject and a verb.)

3. American high school students can choose to study a foreign language. French is very popular, but most students choose Spanish. <u>Because Spanish is already the first or second language for so many Americans</u>.

   Correction: French is very popular, but most students choose **Spanish because** Spanish is already the first or second language for so many Americans today. (Combine two clauses.)

Comma Splice

A comma splice occurs when two or more sentences (clauses) are connected with a comma. One way to correct a comma splice is to separate the clauses by ending the first one with a period and starting the second one with a capital letter. Another correction is to add a connecting word—such as *and, but, or*—after the comma.

Read these comma splices that nonnative speakers wrote. The comma splices are underlined.

1. <u>Last summer I went to Italy, it was a wonderful trip</u>. I want to go again if I can.

   Correction: Last summer I went to Italy. **It** was a wonderful trip.

   or

   Correction: My trip to Italy last summer was wonderful.

2. George Washington was president for eight years. <u>Many people wanted him to continue as president, he refused.</u> This was a very difficult decision for Washington, but it was a very good decision for the country.

    Correction: Many people wanted him to continue as president, **but** he refused.

or

    Correction: **Although** many people wanted him to continue as president, he refused.

3. <u>American high school students can choose to study a foreign language, French is very popular, most students choose Spanish.</u>

    Correction: American high school students can choose to study a foreign language. French is very popular, **but** most students choose Spanish.

Activity 8	Correcting Sentence Fragments and Comma Splices

Read each sentence and decide if it is correct (C) or if it has a sentence fragment (SF) or a comma splice (CS). Write the letter(s) that apply on the first line. If there is an error, circle it and write the corrected sentence(s) on the lines below. More than one correction may be possible. The first one has been done for you.

1. __CS__ American coins are unique in several ways. The dime is the smallest

coin in size, it is not the smallest in monetary value.

The dime is the smallest coin in size, but it is not the smallest in monetary value.

or

The dime is the smallest coin in size. It is not the smallest in monetary value.

2. _____ Yesterday's weather caused problems for many travelers. Most of the flights were canceled.

Due to the torrential rains and high winds.

_____

_____

_____

3. _____ Computer programs can help students learn a foreign language, many students use the

language programs in the computer center.

_____

_____

_____

4. _____ It was definitely a time of nervousness. When the oil embargo was announced, the price of gas-

oline soared. The government did everything possible to make sure that people did not panic.

_____

_____

_____

5. _____ *Family* is a locally produced magazine, the quality of the writing is very high.

_____

_____

_____

6. _____ Last year the magazine won several awards. For the content and the style of its stories.

The last issue had two superb short stories that were written by distinguished authors.

_____

_____

_____

Activity 9   Brainstorming Ideas for a Paragraph

Choose one of the general topics below and brainstorm your ideas in the space provided. When you have finished, circle the ideas that you think are best to include in a paragraph

Topics:

1. The best pet for a child
2. Foods that are good for your health
3. Ways that we can conserve energy
4. How computers are changing society

Brainstorm area:

Activity 10   Original Writing Practice

Use your brainstorming notes from Activity 9 to write a paragraph. Make sure that your paragraph has the four features explained on pages 11–12.

Activity 11   Peer Editing

Work with a partner and exchange paragraphs from Activity 10. Then use Peer Editing Sheet 3 on page 195 to help you comment on your partner's paper. It is important to offer positive comments that will help the writer.

Unit 4

Supporting and Concluding Sentences

GOAL: To learn how to write supporting and concluding sentences

LANGUAGE FOCUS: Using pronouns for key nouns

Now that you know how to write a good topic sentence, you will work on another part of the paragraph—supporting sentences. Consider these questions:

- What is a good supporting sentence?
- What are the different kinds of supporting sentences?
- How do the supporting sentences relate to the topic sentence?

GOOD SUPPORTING SENTENCES

Good supporting sentences are related to the topic sentence and its controlling ideas. Supporting sentences are like the foundation of a house. If a house does not have a good foundation, it will collapse. Likewise, if a paragraph does not have good supporting sentences, its meaning will collapse, and readers will not be able to follow the ideas. The paragraph may be confusing or illogical.

Good supporting sentences give information that supports and explains the topic of the paragraph. They answer questions—*who? what? where? when? why?* and *how?*—and give details. Good writers think of these questions when they write support—that is, supporting sentences—for the topic sentence.

| Activity 1 | Predicting Paragraph Content from Controlling Ideas |

Read each topic sentence and circle the controlling ideas. Then predict the kind of information you will find in the paragraph.

1. *Topic sentence:* One of the best cities to visit on the east coast of the United States is

   Washington, D.C.

   What kind of information do you think is in this paragraph?

   _____

   _____

   _____

2. *Topic sentence:* If you are looking for an interesting career, think about becoming a flight attendant.

   What kind of information do you think is in this paragraph?

   _____

   _____

   _____

3. *Topic sentence:* The person that I most respect and admire is my grandmother Carla.

   What kind of information do you think is in this paragraph?

   _____

   _____

   _____

    As you can see, the topic sentences are all very different. The supporting sentences that you write will depend on your topic sentence.

Activity 2   **Reading Example Supporting Sentences**

Read the paragraphs. Notice how the supporting sentences tell you more about the topic sentence. Compare what you wrote in Activity 1 to the information in each paragraph. How well did you predict the content?

Paragraph 20

A Great Tourist Destination

EXAMPLE PARAGRAPH

One of the best cities to visit on the east coast of the United States is Washington, D.C. It has some of the most interesting landmarks and tourist spots in the country. There are many monuments to visit, such as the Lincoln Memorial, the Jefferson Memorial, and the Washington Monument (the tallest building in Washington). For more excitement, the area called Georgetown in northwest Washington is famous for its shopping, restaurants, and nightclubs. Finally, there is the White House tour. On this tour, people actually walk through many rooms and view the home of the president of the United States. Washington, D.C., is not as large or as famous as New York City, but it has an appeal all its own.

Paragraph 21

A Career in the Sky

EXAMPLE PARAGRAPH

Flight attendants work extremely hard, but they get excellent benefits. Every time they go to work, their scenery changes. Sometimes they get to spend one or two days in a city before flying home. Flight attendants also get bargain prices on airplane tickets for vacations. Imagine spending no more than $10 for any flight in the United States. Finally, flight attendants get to meet a wide variety of people from all over the world. If you are looking for an interesting career, why not consider becoming a flight attendant? Flight attendants can feel good about their jobs because they use their interpersonal skills to help passengers have a safe and comfortable trip.

Paragraph 22

EXAMPLE PARAGRAPH

An Immigrant in the Family

The person that I most respect and admire is my grandmother Carla. She came to the United States from Italy as a baby on a large ship in 1911. Soon after landing at Ellis Island in New York, she began working as a seamstress in Brooklyn. My grandmother survived two world wars, the Great Depression, and a long list of illnesses. Being an immigrant, she also experienced some discrimination. Today, Grandma Carla is still as strong and vivacious as ever, and I love to talk to her and hear her stories every chance that I have.

Notice how each of the supporting sentences relates directly to the topic sentence. Writing good supporting sentences is an important skill that you will work on in this unit.

KINDS OF SUPPORTING SENTENCES

Good writers use many different kinds of supporting sentences. Good supporting sentences:

- *explain:* The family moved from the village to the capital for economic reasons.

- *describe:* She lived in a lovely, three-story castle surrounded by a forest.

- *give reasons:* Larry finally quit his job because of the stressful working conditions.

- *give facts:* More than ten percent of the university's student population is international.

- *give examples:* Oranges and grapefruits grow in Florida.

- *explain:* My grandmother has a samovar. It is a large copper tea urn.

Activity 3	Matching Supporting and Topic Sentences

The two topic sentences below talk about two different diets. Read them, and then read the list of supporting sentences. Match each supporting sentence with the correct topic sentence. Write the topic sentence number on the line. Notice that each sentence is labeled (in parentheses) with the kind of supporting sentence that it is.

Topic sentences

TS 1: Low-fat diets are an excellent way to stay healthy and trim.

TS 2: High-protein diets are favored by athletes and competitors.

Supporting sentences

a. __2__ These foods help build muscles and increase stamina. (fact)

b. __1__ They are preferred by the general public because they help with weight reduction. (reason)

c. _____ Low-fat diets are recommended by most physicians. (fact)

d. _____ Many athletes eat high-protein foods such as meat, beans, and nuts. (example)

e. _____ Low-fat foods include fruits, vegetables, and pasta. (example)

f. _____ Because they are easy to find in stores, low-fat foods are convenient. (reason)

g. _____ Athletes generally use high-protein diets to give them more energy. (reason)

h. _____ Crispy steamed vegetables, grilled fish, meat, and chicken are all tasty parts of a low-fat diet. (description)

| Activity 4 | **Asking Questions about Topic Sentences** |

Read each topic sentence. What information would you expect the writer to include in the paragraph? Write a question that the supporting sentences should answer. Use a who? what? where? when? why? *or* how? *question.*

Example: Smoking should be banned in all public facilities.

Why should smoking be banned?
_____

1. Florida is home to four kinds of poisonous snakes.

_____

2. Classrooms without windows have adverse effects on students.

_____

3. Computer technology will one day eliminate the use of libraries.

_____

4. Learning to play the piano is not as difficult as people think.

_____

5. I will never forget the day my boyfriend broke up with me.

_____

ANALYZING AND WRITING SUPPORTING SENTENCES

In this section you will create topic sentences and then analyze and write some supporting sentences.

| Activity 5 | Brainstorming Topic Sentences |

For each of the general topics in the left column, brainstorm some ideas in the space provided. Then write a topic sentence with controlling ideas in the right column. Underline the controlling ideas. An example has been done for you.

Brainstorming topic	Topic Sentence with Controlling Ideas
Example: vacation • types (summer, honeymoon) • common destinations (national parks, Caribbean islands) • memories (why was it special?)	I will <u>never forget</u> my 1989 <u>summer vacation</u>.

1. mathematics

2. your best friend

3. restaurants

4. a (specific) sport

Activity 6	Asking for More Information

Choose two of your topic sentences from Activity 5 and write them below. Then write four questions about each topic. Remember to use who? what? where? when? why? *or* how? *questions. If you cannot think of four questions, brainstorm some ideas with a classmate. Study this example first.*

Topic Sentence: __The best vacation of my life was during the summer of 1996.__

a. __Why was it the best vacation?__

b. __Where did you go?__

c. __What did you do?__

d. __How old were you at that time?__

Topic Sentence 1. _____

a. _____

b. _____

c. _____

d. _____

Topic Sentence 2. _____

a. _____

b. _____

c. _____

d. _____

You now have a lot of ideas about what to include in your supporting sentences. You may not want to write about all of the ideas, but you have many choices. Remember that the supporting sentences must be related directly to the topic sentence.

| Activity 7 | **Identifying Supporting Sentences** |

Sometimes writers give too much information about the topic. When this happens, the paragraph does not read smoothly, and the reader might get confused about the writer's meaning. *In this activity,* do the following for each paragraph:

- Read the paragraph.
- For each of the underlined, numbered sentences, write *good supporting sentence* or *unrelated sentence* on the corresponding lines below the paragraph.
- Write the reasons for your choices. (One sentence in each paragraph is unrelated to the topic.)

Remember: all the supporting sentences must be related to the topic sentence. The first paragraph has been done for you.

Paragraph 23

Example:

EXAMPLE PARAGRAPH

Rules of Childhood

My parents were very strict with me when I was a child. I think that they were protective because I was an only child. However, at that time it felt like I was in prison. I had to come straight home after school and immediately do my homework. (1) <u>After I finished my homework, I was allowed to watch only one hour of television.</u> While my friends were playing video games or watching cartoons, I was usually doing chores around the house to help my mother. (2) <u>This included doing some of the laundry and ironing, mowing the lawn, and helping to prepare dinner.</u> (3) <u>My father was an architect and my mother was a housewife.</u> Looking back, I am not sorry for all the hard work, but I will probably be less strict with my children.

1. <u>good supporting sentence</u>   It's an example of why I felt I was in prison.

2. <u>good supporting sentence</u>   It's a list of the chores I had to do around the house.

3. <u>unrelated sentence</u>   My parents' occupations are not related to how I was treated.

   There is no relationship between being an architect and being a

   strict parent.

Paragraph 24

EXAMPLE PARAGRAPH

Maintaining Your Pool

Swimming pools can be beautiful, but they need to be maintained every day. First, you must check the amount of chlorine in a swimming pool. (1) <u>If there is not enough chlorine, the pool might begin to grow algae.</u> In addition, you must check the pH level, especially after a rainstorm. Certain chemicals can be added to make sure that the pH level of the pool water is balanced. (2) <u>If you accidentally swallow some of these chemicals, you have to go to the doctor immediately.</u> (3) <u>Finally, you should remove any leaves and small insects that are in the pool.</u> By doing all these things, you can be sure that your pool will last a very long time.

1. _____   _____

   _____

2. _____   _____

   _____

3. _____   _____

   _____

Paragraph 25

EXAMPLE PARAGRAPH

Sweet Dreams

Some people have a hard time falling asleep at night. There are three things that they can do to relax before going to sleep. (1) <u>One of the most pleasant ways to relax is to imagine a beautiful and peaceful place</u>. This requires a creative mind, but it is very effective. Another common method is to practice deep-breathing exercises. These rhythmic exercises are good for getting rid of tension that causes people to stay awake. (2) <u>A third method is to listen to relaxing music such as classical or Baroque music</u>. (3) <u>Baroque music is also popular because it helps students study better</u>. Some people have developed unique ways to help them fall asleep, but these three methods are extremely effective for the majority of problem sleepers.

1. _____   _____

   _____

2. _____   _____

   _____

3. _____   _____

   _____

LANGUAGE FOCUS: Using Pronouns for Key Nouns

Because a paragraph is about one topic, writers often repeat key nouns from the topic sentence in their supporting sentences. However, too much repetition can sound awkward. You can avoid repeating key nouns by replacing them with pronouns after the nouns are first introduced. Study these examples:

One of the best cities to visit on the east coast of the United States is <u>Washington</u>. <u>It</u> has some of the most interesting landmarks and tourist spots in the country.

<u>Flight attendants</u> work extremely hard, but <u>they</u> get excellent benefits. First, every time they go to work, their scenery changes.

The person I most respect and admire is my <u>grandmother Carla</u>. <u>She</u> came to the United States from Italy as a baby on a large ship in 1911.

Consistent Pronoun Use

When you use pronouns, it is important to be consistent. For example, if you use *they* at the beginning of a paragraph, do not switch to *it*. Continue to use the first pronoun throughout the paragraph.

Here is an example. The repeated first pronoun and its possessive form are in italics, and the mistakes in pronoun use are underlined.

> Giraffes are among the most interesting of all the animals that live in Africa. *They* are easily recognized by *their* special features. *They* have long necks and long legs, but <u>its</u> neck is longer than <u>its</u> legs. <u>It</u> usually lives in very dry areas. Fortunately, <u>it</u> can survive a long time without drinking any water. In addition, giraffes have thick eyelashes to protect *their* eyes from the dust in *their* dry habitat.

For practice, write the example paragraph on a separate paper with the correct pronouns.

Activity 8	Identifying Key Nouns and Replacement Pronouns

Read the following sentences. The underlined words are key nouns. Write the correct pronoun for the key noun in the blanks. Use it, they, or we. Study this example:

Example:

<u>Tennis racquets</u> have changed tremendously in the last five years. <u>They</u> used to be small and heavy, but that is no longer true.

1. <u>Soccer</u> is by far the most widely played sport in the world. _____ is played professionally on nearly every continent.

2. I will never forget <u>my brothers Carlos and Juan</u> and what _____ taught me.

3. <u>In-line skating</u> is not only fun, but _____ is also an excellent form of exercise.

4. An interesting thing happened to <u>my classmates and me</u> at school yesterday. _____ were late coming to class, so the teacher yelled at us.

5. If you travel to Budapest, Hungary, you will fall in love with <u>the Danube River</u>. _____ separates the city into two parts, Buda and Pest.

WRITER'S NOTE: Stay on Track

As you write, always look back at your topic sentence. Do not include any information that is unrelated to the topic sentence. It is very easy to lose track of the main idea if you don't refer to the topic sentence from time to time.

GOOD CONCLUDING SENTENCES

Now that you know how to write a good topic sentence and related supporting sentences, it is time to work on another part of the paragraph—the concluding sentence. Consider these questions:

- What is a good concluding sentence?
- What are the different kinds of concluding sentences?
- How do the concluding sentences relate to the topic sentence and to the supporting sentences?

The concluding sentence is the last sentence of the paragraph. Its job is to bring the paragraph to a logical conclusion. For some writers, this is very difficult. One helpful practice is to read many examples of good concluding sentences.

KINDS OF CONCLUDING SENTENCES

There are many different kinds of concluding sentences. We will look at two kinds.

Restate the Main Idea

Perhaps the easiest concluding sentence to write is one that restates the main idea or summarizes the main points of the paragraph.

Examples:

- (Paragraph 4, p. 12) "Although most children want a pet for their family, parents are divided on this issue for a variety of important reasons."

    The information in this concluding sentence is very similar to the topic sentence: *At some point, most parents have to decide whether to allow their children to have pets.* In addition, the concluding sentence includes the phrase "a variety of important reasons" because the paragraph lists several reasons for allowing or not allowing children to have pets.

- (Paragraph 5, p. 14) "Computers have certainly made students' lives much easier."

    This concluding sentence also restates the idea of the topic sentence: *Computers are excellent machines to help students.* The examples in the paragraph show how computers help students in their class work, and the concluding sentence emphasizes this fact.

_____

Make a Prediction

Another common way to end a paragraph is to make a prediction about some aspect of the topic.

Examples:

- (Paragraph 23, page 57) "Looking back, I am not sorry for all the hard work, but I will probably be less strict with my children."

  The writer connects the topic of the paragraph to a future situation related to the topic sentence: *My parents were very strict with me when I was a child.*

- (Paragraph 24, page 58) "By doing all these things, you can be sure that your pool will last a very long time."

  In this paragraph, the writer makes a prediction about your pool if you follow the advice in the topic sentence—*Swimming pools can be beautiful, but they need to be maintained every day*—and the supporting sentences.

ANALYZING AND WRITING CONCLUDING SENTENCES

When you work with the paragraphs in this section, you will also analyze the concluding sentences and revise them if necessary.

| Activity 9 | Paragraph Analysis |

In this activity, do the following for each paragraph:

- Read the paragraph.
- Underline the topic sentence and write TS above it.
- Circle any sentence that is not a good supporting sentence based on the controlling ideas in the topic sentence.
- Underline the concluding sentence two times. If the last sentence is not a good concluding sentence, write a new one on the lines provided.

Paragraph 26

College Adjustments

EXAMPLE PARAGRAPH

When I first started going to college, I was surprised at all the studying I had to do. In high school I hardly ever studied, but my grades were very good. At the university, it seemed that all my professors gave me mountains of homework every night. They all thought that *their* class was the most important! I couldn't watch TV anymore because I had to read pages and pages of information. As a result, my nights out with my friends became limited. I went out only on Saturday nights. It was a big change from high school, where I went out every other night. Although I was surprised at first at the amount of work I had to do, I managed to change my habits and become a very good university student.

_____

_____

Paragraph 27

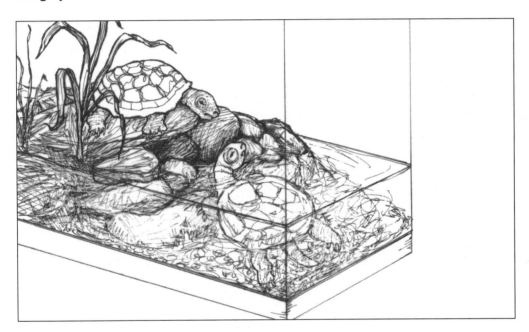

River Turtles

Caring for river turtles is easier than many people think. You don't need a lot of equipment, just a large aquarium, some rocks, sand, and a little bit of vegetation. After you buy the equipment, arrange all the items inside the equipment. Remember to make sure that your river turtles have an area for swimming. If you have a large turtle, you will need to construct a small pond in your back yard. After you have finished these simple steps, your home is ready for your new pet.

_____

_____

Paragraph 28

EXAMPLE PARAGRAPH

Different Ways to Cook Eggs

There are four easy ways to prepare a delicious and nutritious egg. Some people believe that brown eggs taste better than white eggs. The first and probably the easiest way is to boil an egg. Just drop the egg into some water and wait a few minutes for the inside to cook. Another easy way is to scramble an egg. All you need is a fork to beat the egg mixture before you put it into the hot frying pan. A third way is to fry an egg "over easy." This involves breaking the egg into the skillet without breaking the yolk. After a few moments, take a spatula and turn the egg over to cook on the other side. Finally, poaching an egg involves cooking the egg in a small dish that is sitting in boiling water. Break the egg into a small metal cup that is sitting in a pan of very hot, shallow water. Poaching an egg takes only four to five minutes.

_____

_____

Activity 10   **Original Writing Practice**

Choose one of the topic sentences that you wrote in Activity 5 and write a paragraph about the topic. In your supporting sentences, answer the questions that you wrote in Activity 6. Remember: write only about ideas that are introduced in the controlling ideas of your topic sentence. Use the guidelines on page 61 to write a good concluding sentence for your paragraph.

WRITER'S NOTE: Select Important Information

When you write supporting sentences for your paragraph, you as the writer decide what information is important to your meaning.

Activity 11   **Peer Editing**

Work with a partner and exchange paragraphs from Activity 9. Then use Peer Editing Sheet 4 on page 197 to help you comment on your partner's paper. It is important to offer positive comments that will help the writer.

Unit 5

Paragraph Review

GOAL: To review paragraph skills introduced in Units 1–4

LANGUAGE FOCUS: Articles

In the past four units, you have learned about the paragraph. Let's take a moment to review what you have learned.

Features of a Paragraph

These are the four main features of a paragraph:

1. A paragraph has a topic sentence with controlling ideas (main idea).
2. All of the sentences in the paragraph relate to the main topic.
3. The first line of a paragraph is indented.
4. The concluding sentence brings the paragraph to a logical ending.

Language Focus

You have practiced these elements of grammar and punctuation:

- verbs in a sentence
- capitalization and end punctuation
- sentence fragments and comma splices
- pronouns used for key nouns

All these items are important for a good paragraph. In this unit, you will have a chance to use the new information you have learned.

WORKING WITH THE STRUCTURE OF A PARAGRAPH

If you understand how a paragraph is structured, you will be able to write better paragraphs. The activities in this section review the structure of a paragraph.

Activity 1	Writing Topic Sentences

Read each paragraph and write a suitable topic sentence for each one. Remember: the topic sentence contains the controlling ideas related to the supporting sentences. Be sure to add appropriate final punctuation.

Paragraph 29

1. _____

_____

EXAMPLE PARAGRAPH

First, you need to have enough time to request and then submit all the necessary academic records. Often it takes a long time for the records such as transcripts or standardized test scores to arrive at the university. You must be sure that this paperwork reaches the university before the application deadline. Second, the admissions office must have enough time to look at your academic records and decide if you will be accepted. Finally, many universities have a quota, or special number, of students who may enter every semester. If you apply too late, there may not be room for you for the semester in which you want to enter. Following these simple steps can help you get into the university quickly and easily.

Paragraph 30

2. _____

_____

EXAMPLE PARAGRAPH

The Capilano Bridge is listed in the *Guinness Book of World Records* as the world's longest suspension foot bridge. The bridge is 450 feet (137 m) long and rises 230 feet (70 m) above the Capilano River. The original wood and rope bridge was built in 1889 to help loggers cross the steep canyon. However, today only adventure-seeking tourists attempt to cross the narrow, swinging bridge. Unlike the loggers, their goal is not to take trees away from the canyon, but simply to enjoy Canadian nature.

Paragraph 31

3. _____

    _____

EXAMPLE PARAGRAPH
I was very young, and it was the first time my parents let me go out in public without them. I was excited. My friends and I had great seats near the stage. We had to push through crowds of people to get to our seats. As we sat down, the lights dimmed and the crowd grew silent. Then, in a flash of light the band rushed on stage. The guitars blared and the drums crashed. The music was deafening! Everyone in the arena screamed and started to dance. My friends and I didn't sit down all night. The next morning my legs ached and my throat was sore, but I didn't care. I thought attending my first rock concert was the most exciting, grown-up thing I had ever done.

WRITER'S NOTE: Proofread Your Work

Always proofread your work—check it for mistakes. Make sure that you have used correct punctuation and capitalization. Also check to make sure every sentence has a subject and a verb. It is a good idea to have someone else proofread your writing for you, too. Sometimes another reader can see mistakes that you might miss.

Activity 2   **Error Correction in a Paragraph**

The following paragraph contains errors in indentation, capitalization, and punctuation. Read the paragraph and make corrections. There are ten mistakes.

Paragraph 32

How much do you know about hockey? Hockey is a popular sport in both canada and the United states. the game is played on Ice and the players wear skates to move around A hockey player can score a point if he hits a special disk called a Puck into the goal. However, this is not as easy as it seems because each goal is guarded by a special player called a Goalie The goalie's job is to keep the puck away from the goal The next time you see a hockey game on television, perhaps you will be able to follow the action better because you have this information.

Activity 3   **Copying an Edited Paragraph**

After you have made the corrections in Activity 2, write the paragraph here. Think of a title and write it on the line above the paragraph.

_____

_____

_____

_____

_____

_____

_____

_____

Activity 4   **Editing a Paragraph**

The following paragraph contains errors in indentation, capitalization, and punctuation. Read the paragraph and make corrections. There are ten mistakes.

Paragraph 33

Sweet tea is a very easy-to-make drink that is popular in the southern United States. Almost any restaurant in the states of georgia alabama and South carolina will serve this cold beverage To make sweet tea, you must boil a pot of water. once the water boils, add one cup of white sugar to the water. stir the sugar until it dissolves. After that add four tea bags to the pot of water. Let the mixture brew for thirty minutes When the tea is ready, pour it over ice. This sweet drink will definitely refresh you!

| Activity 5 | Copying an Edited Paragraph |

After you have made the corrections in Activity 4, write the paragraph here. Think of a title and write it on the line above the paragraph.

Activity 6   Sequencing Information

These seven sentences are a paragraph, but the sentences are not in the best order. First, read the sentences and number them from 1 to 5 to indicate the best order. In the right column, write the kind of sentence that each one is—topic, supporting, or concluding.

Kind of sentence

a. _____ During ancient Greek and Roman times, when a new ship was built, a small number of coins were left under the mast of the ship. The shipbuilders did this for a very special reason.   _____

b. _____ Today scientists find evidence of this long-standing tradition in a variety of locations, from the decayed remains of old Greek ships to the still active frigate U.S.S. *Constitution*.   _____

c. _____ The art of shipbuilding has some odd traditions, and one of the most interesting of all has its roots in Greek and Roman history.   _____

d. _____ In case of a disaster at sea, the dead crew needed these coins to pay to get to the afterlife. It was believed that sailors without money to cross this river would not be able to take their place in the afterlife.   _____

e. _____ According to legend, the crew members gave these coins to the ferry master Charon to take them across the river Styx to Hades, the land of the dead.

Activity 7   Copying a Paragraph

Create a paragraph by copying the sentences from Activity 6 in their new arrangement. On the top line, write a title for the paragraph.

Paragraph 34

_____

_____

_____

_____

_____

_____

_____

_____

_____

ANALYZING PARAGRAPHS

It helps to notice which sentences work in a paragraph as well as which sentences do not belong.

| **Activity 8** | **Paragraph Analysis** |

Analyze the content and purpose of the paragraph in Activity 7. Read the paragraph again and answer the following questions.

1. What is the topic? _____

_____

2. What is the topic sentence? _____

_____

3. What is the writer's main purpose for writing this paragraph? _____

_____

4. Do you have any ideas for improving this paragraph? _____

_____

WRITER'S NOTE: Check Your Supporting Sentences

Once you have written a paragraph, reread it to make sure that all the supporting sentences relate to the topic sentence. Circle the controlling ideas in the topic sentence to see what each supporting sentence should relate to. For additional help, ask someone to read your paragraph and check the supporting sentences. Another reader may see a mistake that you missed.

Activity 9   **Identifying Good Supporting Sentences**

Read each paragraph. Decide which sentence is not a good supporting sentence. Underline that sentence.

Paragraph 35

EXAMPLE PARAGRAPH

The Frozen North

Due to the harsh climate in the Arctic, very few people live there. Canada, Greenland, Russia, Iceland, Norway, Sweden, and Finland all have large amounts of land in this frozen region, but only a small percentage of their people live in this region. Although these countries have tried to offer incentives for people to move to the Arctic, few go. The scenery is extremely beautiful, but most people cannot get accustomed to the climate there. However, one group of people, the Inuit, has adapted to life in the Arctic. Other people have not been able to do so because life is simply too difficult in this frozen land. England and India do not have any land in the Arctic.

Paragraph 36

Bears of the Arctic

Polar bears have unique bodies that help them live in the harsh weather of the Arctic. They are large animals that weigh up to 1,800 pounds. The body fat from all this weight helps keep them warm. Their heavy, white fur not only protects them from icy winds but also helps them hide in snowdrifts. It snows a lot in the Arctic. The bears have five long, sharp claws on each paw. They use these to walk safely on the ice and to catch their food. Polar bears are truly amazing creatures.

Activity 10   **Proofreading for Comma Errors**

A writing student turned in a paragraph to his teacher. Unfortunately, he didn't proofread it, and it has a lot of comma mistakes.

Proofread the paragraph and help the student get a better grade. Correct the comma mistakes and rewrite the paragraph on the lines provided. Hint: *There are six comma mistakes. (For help with comma errors, see p. 174 in Appendix 3.)*

Paragraph 37

A Great Place to Visit in Florida

Kennedy Space Center is a great place to visit when you are in Florida. There are many exciting things to see and do. First you should visit the Gallery of Space Flight. You can see moon rocks space crafts and space suits there. Next you should visit the Shuttle Plaza and walk through a life-size model of a space shuttle. After that walk to the Astronaut Memorial. Don't forget to watch a movie at the Galaxy Center. Finally you should take a bus tour of the space center and see where the space shuttles are launched. It will be a fun and interesting day!

_____

_____

_____

_____

_____

_____

| Activity 11 | Guided Peer Editing |

A classmate has asked you to proofread her paragraph. She wrote questions in the margin about five things that she is not sure about. Answer the writer's questions and correct the mistakes on her draft. In addition, there are several other mistakes that she could not find. Find these mistakes, too, and correct them on this rough draft.

Paragraph 38

EXAMPLE PARAGRAPH

The Florida Everglades

The Everglades region consists of a unique gigantic freshwater marsh that can be found only in southern florida. Water is vital to this unique environment This region was formed by hundreds of years of flooding from lake Okeechobee after heavy rains these floods always provided the marsh with new water to support its wide variety of plants and animals. Unfortunately people and nature are now taking water away from the Everglades. For example the Miami, Little and New rivers all drain water away from the Everglades. Even worse, man-made dams and canals prevents annual flooding. without this flooding or other source of fresh water, the everglades will eventually die. Only time will tell whether this unique area will be lost to future generations forever.

Should I capitalize lake?

Should I put a period or a comma after rains?

Do I need a comma after Unfortunately?

Do I need to put commas in this list of river names?

Is the verb prevents okay with this subject?

LANGUAGE FOCUS: Articles

The articles *a*, *an*, and *the* are three small words, but they cause many problems for nonnative speakers. It is often difficult to know which article is correct in a sentence. Here are a few guidelines to help you.

1. Always use an article with singular count nouns (SCN).

   Incorrect: My first pet was <u>cat</u>.
   SCN

   Correct: My first pet was <u>a</u> cat.

   Incorrect: Many people believe 13 is unlucky <u>number</u>.
   SCN

   Correct: Many people believe 13 is <u>an</u> unlucky number.

2. When you mean the thing in general, do not use *the*.

   Incorrect: All good chefs know that the <u>salt</u> and the <u>pepper</u> can make food taste better.

   Correct: All good chefs know that salt and pepper can make food taste better.

3. When you mean the thing in general, avoid using *the* + singular count noun. It is more common to use a plural count noun (PCN) without *the*. Notice that the verb also changes from singular to plural.

   Incorrect: The <u>cat</u> is found in many American homes.
   SNC

   Correct: <u>Cats</u> are found in many American homes.
   PCN

4. Use *the* when you refer to a word a second or subsequent time.

   Incorrect: Dinner consisted of steak, potatoes, and carrots. Steak was great, but I didn't like potatoes or carrots.

   Correct: Dinner consisted of steak, potatoes, and carrots. <u>The</u> steak was great, but I didn't like <u>the</u> potatoes or <u>the</u> carrots.

5. Use *the* if there is only one of that thing (unique existence).

   Incorrect: Sun is 93,000,000 miles from our planet.

   Correct: <u>The</u> sun is 93,000,000 miles from our planet.

6. Use *the* when you refer to something specific.

   Incorrect: A bank on corner of Fifty-sixth Street and Fowler Avenue is where Susan works.

   Correct: <u>The</u> bank on <u>the</u> corner of Fifty-sixth Street and Fowler Avenue is where Susan works.

7. Use *the* when you have a superlative form.

   Of all the movies I saw last year, <u>the</u> most interesting was *Cry of the Eagle*.

| Activity 12 | Correcting Articles |

Read this paragraph. Add, delete, or change articles where necessary. Begin with the title.

Paragraph 39

EXAMPLE PARAGRAPH

Best Cook in the World

Beyond a shadow of a doubt,* my grandmother, Florence Folse, is a best cook in world. Many people say that their mother or grandmother can cook a spaghetti or the fried fish or the beans really well. However, if there were cooking contest right now, I'm sure that my grandmother would win. My grandmother has cooked for six children, fifteen grandchildren, twenty-four great-grandchildren, and many more relatives. She cooks from experience. Since my family lives in the southern Louisiana, my grandmother knows how to cook the seafood, the red beans and rice, and the gumbo, which is a kind of seafood soup or stew. Sometimes she uses cookbook, but most of the time she cooks from memory. If you could eat a plate of her fried chicken or meatballs, I'm sure that you would agree with my conclusion about her cooking ability.

---

* **beyond a shadow of a doubt:** without any doubt; 100% certain

Activity 13 · Original Writing Practice

Write a paragraph of five to ten sentences. Choose a general topic and brainstorm a specific idea. Make sure that you have a topic sentence with controlling ideas. After you write your paragraph, check to see if all the supporting sentences are related to the controlling ideas in the topic sentence. Your concluding sentence should restate the topic or make a prediction about it.

Activity 14 · Peer Editing

Work with a partner and exchange paragraphs from Activity 13. Then use Peer Editing Sheet 5 on page 199 to help you comment on your partner's paper. It is important to offer positive comments that will help the writer.

Activity 15 · Additional Writing Assignments

Here are some ideas for paragraphs. Select one of these topics and write an original paragraph. Remember what you have learned in Units 1 through 5. If you need further help, review the writing process in Appendix 1.

1. Write about the worst (or best) day of your life. What happened? When did this happen? Why did this happen? What was the result?

2. What do you think will be the highest-paying occupation fifty years from now? Give reasons to support your opinion.

3. What is the definition of a perfect parent? What are the characteristics of such a person?

4. Choose a mechanical device (for example, a television, a car engine, a fax machine). How does it work? Explain the process step by step.

5. The United Nations was formed in 1945 to promote world peace. However, some people think that the United Nations is useless. Do you think the United Nations is doing a good job? Should the United Nations continue to exist? Why or why not?

Part II

Kinds of Paragraphs

Unit 6

Definition Paragraphs

GOAL: To learn how to write a definition paragraph

LANGUAGE FOCUS: Simple adjective clauses

Like all forms of writing, paragraphs are written for a specific purpose. The purpose determines what information you include in the paragraph and how you write it. In this unit, you will look at one kind of paragraph, the definition paragraph. Definition is a common kind of writing that is easy to understand.

WHAT IS A DEFINITION PARAGRAPH?

A definition paragraph defines something. The word *definition* comes from the verb *to define*, which means "to state the meaning of a word or to describe the basic qualities of something." In a definition paragraph, the writer's main purpose is to tell you what something is.

A definition paragraph

- explains what something is
- gives facts, details, and examples to make the definition clear to the reader

---

The best way to learn what a definition paragraph looks like is to read and study several examples. The three paragraphs that follow are about different topics, but each is an example of a definition paragraph.

Activity 1	Studying Example Definition Paragraphs

Read and study these example paragraphs. Answer the questions.

Paragraph 40

This paragraph is about a kind of food that is common in the southern part of Louisiana. You might write a definition paragraph when you need to explain a special dish or dance or custom from your own country.

Before you read the paragraph, discuss these questions with your classmates.

1. What is seafood? Give three examples.

2. What do you know about the history of Louisiana? Do you know anything about the Cajun people? You may need to consult a dictionary, an encyclopedia, or the Internet.

3. Have you ever seen rice growing? What kind of land is good for growing rice?

4. Have you visited or read about New Orleans? What do you know about this city?

Now read the paragraph.

EXAMPLE PARAGRAPH

Gumbo

The dictionary definition of gumbo does not make it sound as delicious as it really is. The dictionary defines gumbo as a "thick soup made in south Louisiana." However, anyone who has tasted this delicious dish knows that this definition is too <u>bland</u> to describe gumbo. It is true that gumbo is a thick soup, but it is much more than that. Gumbo, one of the most popular of all the <u>Cajun</u> dishes, is made with different kinds of seafood or meat mixed with vegetables <u>such as</u> green peppers and onions. For example, seafood gumbo contains <u>shrimp</u> and <u>crab</u>. Other kinds of gumbo include chicken, sausage, or <u>turkey</u>. <u>Regardless of</u> the <u>ingredients</u> in gumbo, it is always served in a bowl over rice.

Louisiana

bland: not having much taste (good or bad)

Cajun: people who moved from Acadia
   (in Canada) to Louisiana in 1755

such as: like, for example

shrimp: a kind of seafood

crab: a kind of seafood

turkey: a kind of bird that cannot fly
   long distances

regardless of: anyway, no matter

ingredients: food items in a dish

1. What is the topic sentence of this paragraph?

   _____

   _____

2. Write one sentence of your own that tells what gumbo is. Begin "Gumbo is . . ."

   _____

   _____

3. Notice that the writer quotes a dictionary definition of gumbo. Choose one of these food items
   and write a definition in your own words. Do not look in a dictionary.

   sandwich   milk shake   dessert

   hamburger   sundae   pie

   _____

   _____

4. Now look in a dictionary for the definition of the word that you chose in number 3. Write a sentence using that definition. Use the topic sentence in "Gumbo" as a model.

   _____

   _____

5. Is your original definition in number 3 similar to the dictionary definition? If not, how is it different?

_____

_____

Paragraph 41

This paragraph defines something that many people think is wrong, but some people do it anyway. The practice can be harmful.

Before you read the paragraph, discuss these questions with your classmates.

1. What is gossip? Give an example.

2. Is gossip good or bad? Why or why not?

3. Do you think that men gossip less than women do? Explain your answer.

Now read the paragraph.

Gossip

According to *The American Heritage Dictionary*, gossip is a "trivial rumor of a personal nature," but this definition makes gossip sound harmless. At first, gossip might not seem so bad. One person tells a second person something about someone, and that second person tells a third, and so on. The information passes from person to person. However, gossip is much more than just information and rumor. As the rumor continues, it grows and changes. People do not know all the facts. They add information. As the gossip goes from one person to the next person, the damage continues, and the person who is the subject of the gossip can't do anything to answer or protect himself or herself. Because the potential damage may range from hurt feelings to a lost career, gossip is much worse than simply a "trivial rumor."

EXAMPLE PARAGRAPH

trivial: unimportant

rumor: information that is passed
    from person to person

nature: kind, type; characteristics

and so on: etc. (et cetera)

damage: harm

subject: topic or person

potential: possible but not yet actual

range: extent

1. What is the topic sentence of "Gossip"?

_____

_____

2. What is the writer's opinion about gossip? Does the writer think it is wrong? How do you know?

_____

_____

3. Do all the supporting sentences relate to the topic? _____
   Discuss this with a partner.

4. Like the writer of "Gumbo," this writer also quotes a dictionary definition. Read the following sentences. Which ones are easy to read and understand? Which are difficult? Rank them 1 to 4, with 1 being the easiest to read and 4 being the most difficult.

   _____ Paragraph 1: The dictionary defines *gumbo* as a "thick soup made in

   south Louisiana."

   _____ Paragraph 1: The definition of *gumbo* is a "thick soup made in south

   Louisiana."

   _____ Paragraph 2: According to *The American Heritage Dictionary*, gossip is

   a "trivial rumor of a personal nature."

   _____ Paragraph 2: *The American Heritage Dictionary* definition of *gossip* is a

   "trivial rumor of a personal nature."

5. *Gossip* is difficult to define in your own words. Here are some other words that you may find difficult. Choose one, look it up in a dictionary, and write a definition sentence similar to the topic sentence in "Gossip."

   pride   honesty   friendship   luck   fate   patience

_____

_____

_____

Present your sentence to the rest of the class.

Paragraph 42

What is your favorite snack food? This paragraph talks about one kind of snack food that is popular nowadays.

Before you read the paragraph, discuss these questions with your classmates.

1. Write a definition in your own words for *snack*. Compare your definition with other students'.
2. Name three examples of popular snacks.
3. Why do you think these three snacks are so popular?

Now read the paragraph.

EXAMPLE PARAGRAPH

Pretzels

A <u>pretzel</u> is a salted, <u>glazed</u> biscuit that is often shaped or twisted like a <u>knot</u>. The first pretzels were made in an Italian <u>monastery</u> in 610 A.D. These <u>twisted</u> <u>strips</u> of bread were originally called *pretiola*, which means "little <u>reward</u>" in Latin. They were given as <u>treats</u> to local children. The pretzel rapidly became popular throughout Europe. Today the pretzel is an especially popular snack in Germany, Austria, and the United States. As a matter of fact, the current pronunciation of the snack comes from a twisting of the word *pretiola* into the modern English word *pretzel*.

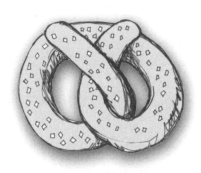

Figure-Eight Knot

pretzel: a snack made of flour

glazed: having a thin, smooth, shiny coating

knot: string tied in loops

monastery: place where members of a religious group live

twisted: turned in several directions

strips: long, thin pieces

reward: something given for a special service or accomplishment

treats: something special

1. Write the topic sentence here.

_____

2. How is this sentence different from the topic sentences in the first two examples?

_____

3. When you write a definition paragraph, you can include a definition from the dictionary or use an original definition. Here are three things that are difficult to define. Choose one and write your own definition.

giraffe   battery   flag

_____

_____

4. Compare your definition with your classmates' definitions. How are they the same? How are they different? Why is yours (or theirs) better?

_____

_____

_____

5. Write an original question and answer about "Pretzels." They can be about the content or about the writing. Work with another student or in small groups and take turns asking and answering your questions.

Question: _____

_____

Answer: _____

_____

WRITER'S NOTE: Quotation Marks

When you write, the ideas and the words are usually your own. However, sometimes you might want to borrow someone else's words. When you use another person's words, you must let the reader know that they are not yours. In English, you do this by putting the borrowed words in quotation marks.

For example, if you use a definition that is taken from another source, such as a dictionary, put the definition inside quotation marks. Look at the second sentence of Paragraph 40, "Gumbo," and the first sentence of Paragraph 41 "Gossip." Both of these sentences include words in quotation marks.

Activity 2 — Adding Quotation Marks

In the following sentences, put quotation marks where necessary. Sometimes you will have to add a comma and capitalize letters. (Remember that commas, periods, and question marks go inside close quotation marks. See p. 173 in Appendix 3 for more information.) Numbers 1 and 6 have been done for you.

words taken from a book

1. The dictionary defines *marriage* as "the union of a husband and a wife."

2. According to *The American Heritage Dictionary*, an errand is a short trip for a specific purpose, but my trip to the courthouse was certainly not a simple errand.

3. If we believe the dictionary definition of *drug* as a narcotic that is addictive, then surely we must say that cigarettes are drugs.

4. The dictionary definition of *opulence*, extremely wealthy or rich, may sound good, but this word does not have a positive meaning for me.

5. Although the dictionary currently defines *a family* as parents and their children, previous definitions probably included additional family members.

words that someone spoke

6. Julie said, "I really hope the vocabulary exam is not too tough. "

7. When all the students were seated, the teacher stood up and announced beginning tomorrow, no student may enter this room wearing any kind of head covering.

8. The taxi driver turned to me and asked where do you want to go?

9. The player stopped the game, approached the net, and calmly asked her opponent are you sure that ball was really out?

10. I can't wait here any longer the man said as he walked out the door.

PUTTING THE PARAGRAPH TOGETHER: SEQUENCING

Good writers create paragraphs with sentences in a certain order for the meaning they want.

| Activity 3 | Sequencing Sentences |

These sentences make one paragraph. Read the sentences and number them from 1 to 7 to indicate the best order.

a. _____ Similarly, an English speaker learning Malay might remember the word *pintu*, which means "door," by using the English words *pin* and *into*.

b. _____ The learner might remember that he or she can use a hatchet eight times to cut down a tree.

c. _____ The key-word method, which can help foreign language learners remember new vocabulary, is gaining popularity among teachers and students.

d. _____ Through these two simple examples, we can get an idea of how useful this method of remembering vocabulary can be.

e. _____ For example, a Japanese learner of English might look at the English word *hatchet* and connect it to the Japanese word *hachi* ("eight") because they sound alike.

f. _____ In this method, learners first form their own sound association between the foreign language word they are trying to learn and a word in their native language. In the second stage, learners form an image link between the target word and the native language word.

g. _____ He or she can imagine putting a pin into the door to open it.

| Activity 4 | Copying a Sequenced Paragraph |

Now copy the sentences from Activity 2 in paragraph form. The result will be a definition paragraph that describes a method for remembering vocabulary. Give the paragraph an original title.

Paragraph 43

_____

_____

_____

_____

_____

_____

_____

_____

_____

_____

_____

Activity 5	Analyzing a Paragraph

The paragraph that you copied in Activity 4 is a definition paragraph. You may want to read it again or refer to it as you complete the answers to these questions.

1. What is the general topic of the paragraph in Activity 4? _____

2. What is the topic sentence? _____

   _____

3. What is the writer's main purpose for writing this paragraph?

   _____

4. How many examples are given in the supporting sentences? _____

   List them here: _____

   _____

   _____

   _____

5. If Paragraph 43 did not have any examples, how would that affect your understanding of the information?

   _____

   _____

   _____

6. Can you think of two more examples?

   _____

   _____

WRITER'S NOTE: Include Examples

Good writers include examples, especially when they are writing about a difficult or abstract topic.

When to Use an Example

How do you know when to use an example? Consider your readers. If you think they already know something about your topic, then you do not have to give many examples, details, or facts. However, if the topic may be new to many readers, it is helpful to include some supporting information.

Where to Put an Example

Where should you put examples in the paragraph? The best place to put an example is usually just after you have explained an idea. If your paragraph compares two ideas, explain both ideas first, then provide examples of both in the next sentence.

How to Begin an Example

How should you begin a sentence with an example? You might write, "For example, . . ." or "An example of this is . . ." You can also write an example sentence without such an introduction. In the following sentences, the example sentence is underlined.

Different cultures have different superstitions, but all cultures have some kind of superstition. People might believe that a certain number is lucky or unlucky. <u>Many North Americans think 7 is a lucky number, but the Chinese believe 4 is unlucky.</u>

LANGUAGE FOCUS: Simple Adjective Clauses

A simple adjective clause is made up of a relative pronoun (*that, which, who*) followed by a verb and sometimes an object. It describes the noun(s) that comes before it. Study these examples:

ADJECTIVE CLAUSE

Gumbo is a thick <u>soup</u>   <u>that</u>   <u>contains</u>   <u>seafood or meat</u>.
    NOUN   RELATIVE PRONOUN   VERB   OBJECTS

ADJECTIVE CLAUSE

A goalie is a <u>soccer player</u>   <u>who</u>   <u>protects</u>   <u>his team's goal</u>.
    NOUN   RELATIVE PRONOUN   VERB   OBJECT

Notes:

- Use *that* or *which* for things. (*That* is more common.)

- Use *who* or *that* for people. (*Who* is preferred.)

Let's look more closely at two examples:

Gumbo   is a thick   <u>soup</u>   <u>that contains seafood or meat</u>.
SPECIFIC NOUN   GENERAL NOUN   ADJECTIVE CLAUSE

Samba   is a rhythmic   <u>dance</u>   <u>that is popular in Brazil</u>.
SPECIFIC NOUN   GENERAL NOUN   ADJECTIVE CLAUSE

In a definition, the specific noun (*gumbo, Samba*) is the word you are defining. The general noun (*soup, dance*) is the group that the specific noun belongs to. The relative pronoun (*that*) refers to both nouns.

| Activity 6 | Recognizing Simple Adjective Clauses |

Read the next paragraph. Underline all the adjective clauses. Look for the relative pronouns that, which, *and* who. *Circle the noun that each clause modifies or describes. The first one is done for you.*

Paragraph 44

Nature's Worst Storm

EXAMPLE PARAGRAPH

A hurricane is a dangerous (storm) that features high winds and heavy rains. In addition, areas along the coast may experience a tidal surge that can flood whole towns. Hurricanes in the Atlantic Ocean occur mostly between April and November. However, the months which have the most hurricanes are August and September. Modern technology has now made it possible for people who live in a given area to know in advance if there is danger of a hurricane striking their region. However, this was not always the case. For example, a hurricane that surprised the residents of Galveston, Texas, in 1900 resulted in thousands of deaths. Though we know much more about hurricanes now and can track their movements, hurricanes continue to be one of the most dangerous weather phenomena.

| Activity 7 | Writing Sentences with Simple Adjective Clauses |

Write a definition for each term. Include an adjective clause in your definition and underline the clause. An example has been done for you.

1. turtle

    A turtle is a slow-moving, four-legged animal <u>that goes inside its shell when there is danger</u>.

2. copilot

    _____

    _____

3. skunk

    _____

    _____

4. passport

    _____

    _____

5. submarine

    _____

    _____

6. odd numbers

    _____

    _____

7. Thomas Edison

    _____

    _____

8. plumber

_____

_____

9. Neil Armstrong

_____

_____

10. the United Nations

_____

_____

Share your sentences with a partner. Did your partner include an adjective clause in each definition?

WRITER'S NOTE: Combine Sentences for Variety

One way to improve your writing is to write different kinds of sentences. Many beginning writers use only simple sentences that have a subject, a verb, and an object. For variety, combine two short sentences with a connecting word, such as *and, but, or,* and *so.*

Simple sentences:	I studied math for five hours last night. I failed the test.
Combined sentence:	I studied math for five hours last night, *but* I failed the test.
Simple sentences:	The scientist forgot to control the temperature. The experiment was not successful.
Combined sentence:	The scientist forgot to control the temperature, *so* the experiment was not successful.

Examples of Sentence Variety

In addition, good writers use adjectives, adjective clauses, adverbs, adverb clauses, prepositional phrases, and other variations in their sentences. Study these examples. The variations are underlined.

Adjectives

Simple sentence:	The manager rejected the schedule.
Variation:	The <u>current</u> <u>business</u> manager rejected <u>Mark's</u> <u>revised</u> schedule.

Adjective clauses

Simple sentence:	The students liked the suggestion.
Variation:	The students <u>who are in charge of planning the</u> <u>party</u> liked the suggestion <u>that Mark made</u>.

Adverbs

Simple sentence:	The woman picked up the chain saw.
Variation:	<u>Next</u>, the woman <u>carefully</u> picked up the chain saw.

Adverb clauses

Simple sentence:	He asked her to sit down.
Variation:	<u>Before the doctor told the woman the news</u>, he asked her to sit down.

Prepositional phrases

Simple sentence:	I did all the homework.
Variation:	I did all the homework <u>on my computer</u> <u>in about</u> <u>three hours</u>.

Reading for sentence variety

Read the next two paragraphs. Do you notice any difference in the writing styles? Discuss your impression of each paragraph with a partner.

Example 1: I was walking on Stern Street. I was in front of the bank. I heard a bang. It was loud. It was violent. The front door of the bank opened. This happened suddenly. A boy left the bank. He did this hurriedly. He was tall. He was very thin. He had wavy hair. It was brown. He had a gun. It was silver. It was shiny. It was in his right hand.

Example 2: I was walking in front of the bank on Stern Street. Suddenly I heard a loud, violent bang, and the front door of the bank opened. A tall, very thin boy with wavy brown hair hurriedly left from the bank. In his right hand, he had a shiny, silver gun.

Perhaps you noted that Example 1 has seventeen sentences, and Example 2 has only four sentences. However, both examples include the same information. Example 1 has short, choppy sentences, which make reading uneven and difficult. In Example 2, the writer has combined phrases and ideas together to make more complex sentences that sound better and read more smoothly.

Activity 8	**Sentence Combining**

Each paragraph is missing a sentence. Create the missing sentence from the sentences below the paragraph. Use all the ideas, but not necessarily all the words. Make one sentence. It should be a good supporting sentence. Write the new sentence on the blank lines in the paragraph.

Paragraph 45

EXAMPLE PARAGRAPH

Patience

Patience means the ability to continue doing something even if you do not see any results immediately. We can see patience in a teacher who works with young children. She may not be feeling very well that day, but she smiles and does not get angry when a child misbehaves. We can see patience in a clerk who is polite to a customer even though the clerk has already been at work for seven or eight hours. _____

_____

_____

_____ . In our modern society, people often lack simple patience. People nowadays often expect immediate results all the time. To me, patience is one mark of a civilized society.

We can see patience in a person.   The person is at a street corner.
The person is waiting.   It is beginning to drizzle.

Paragraph 46

EXAMPLE PARAGRAPH

Seward's Folly

A folly is a costly action that has a bad or an absurd result. Did you know that the purchase of Alaska, which is the largest oil-producing state in the United States, was once considered a folly? In fact, Alaska was called "Seward's Folly." This name refers to Secretary of

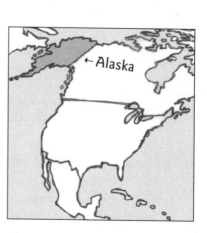

EXAMPLE PARAGRAPH

State William Seward, who convinced Congress that buying Alaska from Russia in 1867 was a good idea. At that time, many Americans thought that it was a waste of money to buy a cold, barren land for several million dollars. However, they were wrong.

_____

_____ . Large amounts of gold and other minerals have been found in Alaska. Alaska is an important source of oil for the United States. In addition, thousands of people visit Alaska each year to see the natural beauty of the state. The purchase of Alaska in 1867 may have seemed like a bad decision at the time, but today we know that buying Alaska was certainly not a folly.

Alaska is not a cold place all the time.
Alaska is not a barren place all the time.
It was not a waste of money.

Paragraph 47

An Unusual Word Relationship

EXAMPLE PARAGRAPH

You might never guess that the words *pottery* and *sincere* are related. *Sincere* comes from two Latin words: *sin* meaning "without," and *cere* means "wax." Thus, *sincere* means "without wax." _____

_____

_____ . It took a long time to make this pottery, and occasionally the pottery would have cracks in it. Pottery with a crack in it was worthless and had to be destroyed. Some potters who did not want to make brand-new pottery would put wax on the crack. To the eye of the careless shopper, the pottery looked good. However, people soon realized which potters were good and which were not good. Thus, the most respected potters made pottery that was without wax, or "sincere," and that is how the word *sincere* began.

People used pottery.   The pottery was for plates.
This was in ancient times.   The pottery was for bowls.
The pottery was made of clay.

Hint: Begin with a time phrase.

Activity 9

Original Writing Practice

Write a definition paragraph. Follow these guidelines:

- Choose a topic.

- Brainstorm some information about the topic. What do you want to include? What do your readers know about the topic? What do they want to know?

- Write a topic sentence with controlling ideas.

- Write a few supporting sentences that relate to the topic.

- End with a concluding sentence that restates the topic or makes a prediction about it.

- If you use words from another source, put quotation marks around them.

If you need help, study the example definition paragraphs in this unit. Be sure to refer to the seven steps in the writing process in Appendix 1 on pages 160–168.

Activity 10

Peer Editing

Work with a partner and exchange paragraphs from Activity 9. Then use Peer Editing Sheet 6 on page 201 to help you comment on your partner's paper. Remember that it is important to offer positive comments that will help the writer.

Activity 11

Additional Writing Assignments

Here are some ideas for definition paragraphs. When you write your paragraph, follow the guidelines in Activity 9.

1. Choose an emotion such as love or jealousy. How does the dictionary define it? Is it a good emotion or a bad emotion? Who usually feels this emotion and why? Give some examples.

2. Choose a scientific or medical term, such as *gravity, tides, molecule, appendix, AIDS,* or *pediatrics.* What is it? Why is it important?

3. Write a paragraph in which you define the word *censorship.* What is it? What is its purpose? Who does this? For what reason? Is it acceptable? If so, are there any limitations?

4. Write about a word that is borrowed from another language. Examples are *coup d'état, siesta,* and *sushi.* What is it? What language does the word come from? What do the words mean in that language? How long has the word been widely used in English?

5. What is freedom? Why do people want it? Should there be limitations on freedom? Can there be limitations? Explore the nature of freedom.

Unit 7

Process Analysis Paragraphs

GOAL: To learn how to write a process analysis paragraph

LANGUAGE FOCUS: Transition words and chronological order

W hat did you do to get ready for class today? Think about what you did first, then second, and so on. Perhaps you woke up and took a shower. After that, maybe you got dressed and combed your hair. What did you do next? You completed a process to prepare yourself to come to class.

The world is full of processes. At times, you are required to describe how to do something or how something works or happens. You can often use a process analysis paragraph to convey the information.

WHAT IS A PROCESS ANALYSIS PARAGRAPH?

In a process analysis paragraph, you divide a process into separate steps. Then you list or explain the steps in chronological, or time, order. Special time words or phrases allow you to tell the reader when a particular step occurs. The process analysis paragraph ends with a specific result—something that happens at the end of the process.

> A process analysis paragraph
>
> • explains a sequence or process
>
> • presents facts and details in chronological order
>
> • uses time words or phrases
>
> • ends with a specified result

The best way to learn what a process analysis paragraph looks like is to read and study several examples. The three paragraphs that follow are about different topics, but each is an example of a process analysis paragraph.

| Activity I | **Studying Example Process Analysis Paragraphs** |

Read and study these example paragraphs. Answer the questions.

Paragraph 48

The topic of this paragraph is a popular Mexican dish. People have to be careful when they eat this food because it can be messy.

Before you read the paragraph, discuss these questions with your classmates.

1. What are some Mexican food dishes? Do you know the ingredients? If so, what are they?

2. Are any of these foods messy when you eat them? If so, what makes them messy?

3. Name a food that you ate that was very messy. Why was this particular food messy?

Now read the paragraph.

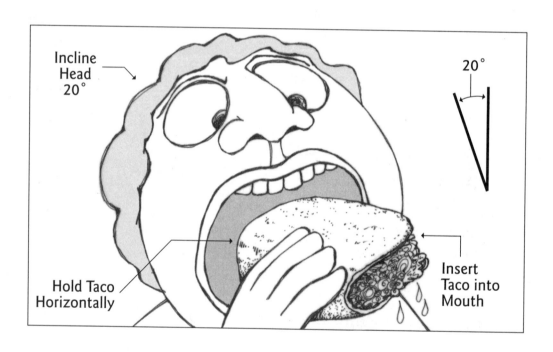

A Popular but <u>Messy</u> Food

EXAMPLE PARAGRAPH

Eating a juicy <u>taco</u> is not easy—it requires following <u>specific</u> directions. First, you must be sure you are wearing clothes that you don't mind getting dirty. Eating a taco while you are wearing an expensive <u>silk</u> blouse is not a smart idea. The next thing that you should do is to decide if you want to eat the taco alone or in front of others. Eating a taco in front of someone you do not know very well, such as a new date, can be <u>embarrassing</u>. The last step is to plan your attack! It is a good idea to pick up the taco gently and carefully keep it in a <u>horizontal</u> position. As you raise the taco, slowly turn your head toward it and position your head at a twenty-degree <u>angle</u>. The last step is to put the corner of the taco in your mouth and bite. By following these simple directions, eating a taco can be a <u>pleasant</u> experience.

messy: not neat

taco: a Mexican dish consisting
    of a corn tortilla wrapped
    around a mixture of ground
    beef, lettuce, tomato, cheese,
    and sauce

specific: exact

silk: a kind of cloth made from
    thread produced by silk worms

embarrassing: causing a self-conscious
    or uncomfortable feeling

horizontal: across, from side to side
    (opposite: vertical)

angle: where two lines meet

pleasant: nice

1. What is the topic sentence of this paragraph?

_____

_____

2. This paragraph discusses three things about eating tacos. What are they?

    a. _Don't wear expensive clothes because you might spill something on them._ ___

    _____

    _____

    b. _____

    _____

    _____

    c. _____

    _____

    _____

3. Do you think these instructions for eating a taco are correct? Is there anything that should
    be added?

_____

_____

Paragraph 49

This paragraph is about the steps involved in applying to an American university.

Before you read the paragraph, discuss these questions with your classmates.

1. What are the steps in applying to a university in the United States?

2. What are the steps in applying to a university in your country?

3. Is it difficult to enter the university in your country? How does it compare with entering a university in the United States?

Now read the paragraph.

EXAMPLE PARAGRAPH

Applying to an American University

Although the process for applying to an American university is not <u>complicated</u>, it is important to follow each step. The first step is to choose several schools that you are interested in attending. Next, write to these schools to ask for information, <u>catalogues</u>, and applications. You may also want to visit the schools' <u>Web sites</u>. After you have <u>researched</u> several schools, <u>narrow</u> your list to three to five. Then mail all the required forms and documents only to your final list of three to five schools. If the school of your choice requires you to take a standardized test such as the <u>SAT</u> or <u>ACT</u>, be sure to do so early. In addition, ask various school officials and teachers to write letters of recommendation for you if the university requires them. Finally, almost all schools have an application <u>fee</u>. This should be sent in the form of a check or money order. One last piece of advice is to start early because thousands of high school students are all applying at the same time.

complicated: difficult, complex

catalogues: information booklets

Web sites: locations of information on the World Wide Web (www)

researched: investigated

narrow: limit; reduce

SAT: Scholastic Aptitude Test

ACT: American College Test

fee: a required payment

1. What is the topic sentence of this paragraph?

_____

_____

2. What is the author's main suggestion for a successful application process?

_____

_____

3. Does the paragraph explain the difference between the ACT and the SAT? Why or why not?

_____

_____

4. According to the information in this paragraph, how many steps are there? _____ Which of the steps has two parts? Write them here.

_____

_____

Paragraph 50

This paragraph is about another kind of food, but it tells how to make the food instead of how to eat it. It describes how to make a kind of beverage from Turkey.

Before you read the paragraph, discuss these questions with your classmates.

1. What are some of the most popular beverages? Are they served hot or cold? Are they easy or difficult to prepare?

2. Have you ever visited Turkey? What information do you know about this country?

3. Can you name any popular beverages that come from Turkey?

Now read the paragraph.

EXAMPLE PARAGRAPH

A <u>Unique</u> Treat

Turkish coffee is not easy to make, but the <u>results</u> are delicious. First, you need a special coffeepot called a *jezve*. This is a long-handled, open <u>brass</u> or <u>copper</u> pot. <u>Pour</u> three small cups of water into the pot. Next, heat the water until it <u>boils</u>. Then <u>remove</u> the pot from the heat. Add three teaspoons of coffee and three teaspoons of sugar to the water. Gently <u>stir</u> the mixture and return it to the heat until you can see <u>foam</u> on the top. When you can see the foam on top, take the *jezve* from the heat and hit it lightly with a spoon to make the foam go down. Reheat the coffee and tap the pot two more times, making sure to remove it from the heat each time the foam forms. Before you serve the coffee, give everyone a small glass of fresh water to drink with their hot, thick coffee.

unique: different from all others

results: the product of an action

brass: a gold-colored metal

copper: a reddish-gold metal

pour: let something flow from one container to another

boils: bubbles rapidly because of heat

remove: take away

stir: mix

foam: liquid with a lot of tiny air bubbles in it

1. List the first five steps in making Turkish coffee.

    a. _Get the special pot._ _____

    b. _____

    c. _____

    d. _____

    e. _____

2. The process of making Turkish coffee includes more than ten small steps. Good writers don't always write one sentence for each small step. Instead, they combine some steps in longer sentences. Write a sentence from the paragraph that has more than one step in it.

    _____

3. Combine these two steps in one sentence: *Pour three small cups of water into the pot. Next, heat the water until it boils.*

    _____

    _____

4. The author states that Turkish coffee is difficult to make. Find three examples from the paragraph that support this idea.

    a. _____

    b. _____

    c. _____

ORGANIZING A PROCESS ANALYSIS PARAGRAPH

The order of steps in a process is important to the success of a process analysis paragraph.

WRITER'S NOTE: Use Index Cards to Help You Organize

It is important that all the steps in your process analysis paragraph be in the correct order. A simple way for you to organize the steps is to write each one on a 3-by-5 index card. This will allow you to arrange and rearrange them. It will also help point out any steps that may be missing.

LANGUAGE FOCUS: Transition Words and Chronological Order

A process analysis paragraph is usually arranged in *chronological* (time) order. In other words, the steps in the process are listed in the order that they occur in time. The three paragraphs in Activity 1 each describe how to do or make something. The writers use chronological order to show the reader when the steps in the process occur.

Writers use *time phrases*, *time clauses*, and *time words* to show time order in a process. These are also called *transition words* because they mark the transition from one step to the next.

1. Study the time/transition words in the following list. In the right column are examples of how they are used in the paragraphs in Activity 1.

Time/transition words	Examples
Then	Then remove the water . . .
First, (Second, Third, etc.)	First, you must be sure . . .
Next, (The next step/thing)	The next thing you should do is decide . . .
The last step (Finally,)	The last step is to insert the corner . . .
Before	Before you serve the coffee . . .
After	After the foam forms . . .

2. Now turn back to paragraph 49 and circle all the transition words that you can find. Notice that some time phrases and words are followed by a comma when they appear at the beginning of a sentence. Time clauses (*After you have researched several schools,*) are always followed by a comma when they appear at the beginning of a sentence.

Activity 2   Sequencing Sentences

The following sentences make up a paragraph. Number them from 1 to 8 to indicate the best order. Then underline all the time words or phrases.

a. _____ Hit the ball into the small box on the opposite side of the net.

b. _____ After you hit the ball, continue swinging your racket down and across the front of your body.

c. _____ Just before the ball reaches its peak, begin to swing your racket forward as high as you can reach.

d. _____ First, toss the ball with your left hand about three feet in the air. The best position for the ball is just to the right of your head.

e. _____ At the same time, move your racket behind your shoulder with your right hand so that your elbow is pointed at the sky.

f. _____ After you have completed the serve, your racket should be near your left knee.

g. _____ Many people think serving in tennis is difficult, but the following steps show that it is quite easy.

h. _____ If you are left-handed, you should substitute the words *left* and *right* in the preceding directions.

Activity 3   Sequencing Information in Paragraph Form

Copy the sentences from Activity 2 in paragraph form. The result will be a process analysis paragraph. Give the paragraph an original title.

Paragraph 51

_____

_____

_____

_____

_____

_____

_____

_____

_____

| Activity 4 | **Analyzing and Understanding a Paragraph** |

The paragraph in Activity 3 is a process analysis paragraph. You may want to read it again or refer to it as you complete the answers to these questions.

1. What is the general topic of the paragraph in Activity 3?

   _____

2. What is the topic sentence?

   _____

   _____

3. The main purpose of this paragraph is to explain how to serve a tennis ball. However, the author also expresses an opinion in the topic sentence. Read the topic sentence again. What is that opinion?

   _____

   _____

4. Look at this sentence from the paragraph: "The best position for the ball is just to the right of your head." Unlike the other sentences, this is not a step. What is the purpose of this sentence?

_____

_____

WRITER'S NOTE: Define Technical Terms

Consider your readers when you write a process analysis paragraph. Ask yourself this question: *How much do the readers already know about my subject?* If they don't have much information about your topic, you will need to use simple, clear terms to describe your steps. In your rough draft, underline all the technical terms you use. This will remind you to rephrase them or write a simple definition when you use them.

Activity 5   Commas and Time Phrases

Transitional words, phrases, and clauses can show chronological order. Most transitional words and clauses are followed by a comma. (Refer to page 105 for more information if you need help.)

The following sentences make up a paragraph. Number them from 1 to 10 to indicate the best order. In addition, add commas where necessary. Hint: There are five mistakes.

a. _____ First put the water and the plants in the jar.

b. _____ One week later check the fish.

c. _____ The fact that the fish is still alive shows that oxygen was added. If you look carefully at a plant stem when it is in sunlight, you can see the tiny bubbles of oxygen escaping from the plant.

d. _____ When you do this be sure to leave about an inch of empty space.

e. _____ Keep the jar in a cool place indoors, but be sure that it receives some direct sunlight for a few hours each day.

f. _____ When you are sure that the water in the jar is at room temperature add the fish.

g. _____ Here is a simple science experiment that proves that plants produce oxygen.

h. _____ For this experiment, you will need a clean quart jar with a tight lid, some

tape, a goldfish, some water, and a few green plants.

i. _____ Put the lid on as tightly as you can.

j. _____ After that wrap the lid with several layers of tape so that you are sure no

air can pass through it.

Activity 6   **Writing a Paragraph with Time Words**

The sentences in Activity 5 explain the steps of a simple science experiment. After you have made the comma corrections and arranged the sentences in the correct order, write the completed process analysis paragraph on the lines below. Create a title for the paragraph.

Paragraph 52

_____

_____

_____

_____

_____

_____

_____

_____

_____

WRITER'S NOTE: Check Possessive Adjectives

When you write a sentence, you sometimes use possessive adjectives to refer to nouns or pronouns that have come before. Check to see if these possessive adjectives refer correctly to the noun or pronoun that they represent. Be careful with singular and plural usage.

Incorrect: <u>One</u> of the parent penguins keeps the egg on one of <u>their</u> feet at all times.

Correct: <u>One</u> of the parent penguins keeps the egg on one of <u>its</u> feet at all times.

If you have trouble with possessive adjective reference, circle all the possessive adjectives in your rough draft. Underline the nouns or pronouns to which they refer. Check for correctness. You may also want to ask a reader to check your draft for correct possessive adjective reference.

| **Activity 7** | **Sentence Combining Practice** |

In each item below, combine the information in all the sentences to make one good sentence. It is not necessary to use all the words from the sentences, but you must use all of the ideas in your new sentence. You may need to use these connecting words: and, because, such as, when, or, according to.

This coffee is hot.   It is difficult to make.   This coffee is thick.

1. _____

   _____

A *jezve* is a coffeepot.   It doesn't have a lid.   It has a long handle.

2. _____

   _____

Jenny has a sunburn.   She was at the beach.
The sunburn is very painful.   Jenny fell asleep.

3. _____

   _____

The children watched the cartoon.   The cartoon was funny.
They watched the cartoon on Saturday morning.   The children were sleepy.

4. _____

   _____

You eat a taco.

You must turn your head to eat a taco.

You must turn your head slowly.

You must turn your head toward the taco.

You must turn your head at a twenty-degree angle.

5. _____

_____

Activity 8   Original Writing Practice

Write a process analysis paragraph. Follow these guidelines:

- Choose a topic.
- Write some notes about the steps in the process.
- Write a topic sentence with controlling ideas.
- Write supporting sentences that give the steps in chronological order. Use transition words to make sure the steps are in the correct order.

If you need help, study the example process analysis paragraphs in this unit. Be sure to refer to the seven steps in the writing process in Appendix 1 on pages 160–168.

Activity 9   Peer Editing

Work with a partner and exchange paragraphs from Activity 8. Then use Peer Editing Sheet 7 on page 203 to help you comment on your partner's paper. It is important to offer positive comments that will help the writer.

Activity 10   Additional Writing Assignments

Here are some ideas for process analysis paragraphs. When you write your paragraph, follow the guidelines in Activity 8.

1. What do you need to do to get a driver's license?
2. Describe how to make a food dish.
3. What steps does a successful job applicant follow?
4. How would you propose to your boyfriend or girlfriend?
5. Describe how to explore the World Wide Web.

Unit 8

Descriptive Paragraphs

GOAL: To learn how to write a descriptive paragraph

LANGUAGE FOCUS: Adjectives; denotation and connotation

You use description every day. You might describe to a friend how you feel or what you had for lunch. In description, you tell someone what something looks or feels like. What descriptions have you used today?

WHAT IS A DESCRIPTIVE PARAGRAPH?

A descriptive paragraph describes how something or someone looks or feels. It gives an impression of something. If you only wanted to explain to someone what a *samovar* is, for example, you could write a *definition* paragraph because a definition paragraph does not include how the writer feels. However, if you wanted to tell about the feelings you had when you drank a cup of Russian tea that was made in a samovar, you would write a *descriptive* paragraph.

Read this example descriptive paragraph.

Paragraph 53

EXAMPLE PARAGRAPH

Samovar Memory

Every time I have a cup of strong Russian tea, I remember my sweet grandma and her magical samovar. When I was a little girl, my grandmother would make tea for me in this giant, gleaming tea urn. I was fascinated by the samovar and its tasty contents. Its copper sides were decorated with beautiful red and black swirls. Grandma told me that the intricate decorations were painted by skilled craftsmen from her village. I can still remember the smell of the dark tea that my grandma made using the urn. Its leaves always filled her tiny apartment with an exotic aroma, and the rich brew tasted like liquid velvet.

A descriptive paragraph

- describes
- gives impressions, not definitions
- "shows" the reader
- creates a sensory* image in the reader's mind

*related to the five senses: hearing, taste, touch, sight, smell

DESCRIBING WITH THE FIVE SENSES

Good writers use words that appeal to some or all of the five senses—sight, taste, touch, hearing, and smell—to help describe a topic. Here is a list of the senses and examples of what they can describe. Add examples of your own under Example 2.

Sense	Example 1	Example 2
Sight	a sunset	_____
Taste	wedding cake	_____
Touch	silk	_____
Hearing	a baby's cry	_____
Smell	perfume	_____

Activity 1   **Using Adjectives to Describe Sensory Information**

Write your five examples from the list above in the left column. In the right column, write three adjectives that describe each object. Try to use different senses. One has been done for you as an example.

Example	Description
Sunset	purple, streaked, majestic
1. _____	_____
2. _____	_____
3. _____	_____
4. _____	_____
5. _____	_____

| Activity 2 | **Writing Sentences Using Sensory Adjectives** |

Use the five topics from Activity 1. For each one write a descriptive sentence using one or more of the adjectives you wrote. Share your sentences with a classmate.

1. _____

   _____

2. _____

   _____

3. _____

   _____

4. _____

   _____

5. _____

   _____

The best way to learn what descriptive paragraphs look like is to read and study several examples. The three paragraphs that follow are about different topics, but each is an example of a descriptive paragraph.

| Activity 3 | **Studying Example Descriptive Paragraphs** |

Read and study these example paragraphs. Answer the questions.

Paragraph 54

This first paragraph describes the sights, smells, and sounds of a subway station.

Before you read the paragraph, discuss these questions with your classmates.

1. What is a subway? What is its purpose?
2. Where do you usually find a subway?
3. What kinds of people use the subway?
4. Have you ever been on a subway? How did you feel when you rode on it?
5. What did you see, smell, and hear?

Now read the paragraph.

Underground Events

The subway is an <u>assault</u> on your senses. You walk down the steep, <u>smelly</u> staircase onto the subway <u>platform</u>. On the far right wall, a broken clock shows that the time is four-thirty. You wonder how long it has been broken. A mother and her crying child are standing to your left. She is trying to clean dried chocolate <u>syrup</u> off the young child's face. Farther to the left, two old men are <u>arguing</u> about the most recent tax increase. You hear a little noise and see some paper trash roll by like a soccer ball. The most interesting thing you see while you are waiting for your subway train is a poster. It reads "Come to Jamaica." Deep blue skies, a lone palm tree, and <u>sapphire</u> waters call you to this exotic faraway place.

assault: attack

smelly: a bad or unpleasant smell

platform: raised area

syrup: thick liquid

arguing: verbal fighting

sapphire (*adj.*): dark blue

1. What does this paragraph describe?

   _____

2. Can you think of other places where people wait for something?

   _____

   _____

3. Which of the five senses does the writer use to describe this place? Give examples from the paragraph to support your answers.

_____

_____

_____

4. What verb tense is used in this paragraph? Why do you think the writer uses that tense?

_____

_____

Paragraph 55

This paragraph describes a memory about a dangerous kind of weather.

Before you read the paragraph, discuss these questions with your classmates.

1. What are some dangerous kinds of weather?
2. Have you ever experienced these kinds of weather? How did you feel?
3. When you think of these kinds of weather, what sensory adjectives come to mind?

Now read the paragraph.

EXAMPLE PARAGRAPH

Danger from the Sky

The long, slender <u>tornado</u> began to descend from the <u>swirling</u> clouds. When the deadly <u>funnel</u> finally touched the ground, pieces of <u>debris</u> were <u>hurled</u> through the air. The tornado <u>ripped</u> the roof from an old house and threw the contents of the home across the neighborhood. All the while, the tornado's <u>ferocious</u> winds <u>roared</u> like a wild beast. It was hard to believe that something that looked so <u>delicate</u> could cause so much destruction.

tornado: a rotating column of air that moves at very high speeds

swirling: rotating or spinning

funnel: a cone-shaped object

debris: broken pieces of something

hurled: thrown with great force

ripped: torn roughly

ferocious: very wild and savage

roared: made a loud, deep, long sound

delicate: fragile

1. What does this paragraph describe?

_____

2. What verb tense does the writer use in this paragraph? _____

   Choose five verbs and change them to *simple present tense*.

   _____

   _____

3. Which of the five senses does the writer use to describe this kind of weather? Give some examples to support your answer.

   _____

   _____

4. One of the features of a good descriptive paragraph is the use of adjectives that help the reader feel the situation. List any five adjectives in "Danger from the Sky." Then write the feelings they describe.

Adjective	Feelings
a. _____	_____
b. _____	_____
c. _____	_____
d. _____	_____
e. _____	_____

Paragraph 56

The next paragraph describes what the writer's mother did while she worked in her garden. Notice how often the writer appeals to the senses of sight and touch.

Before you read the paragraph, discuss these questions with your classmates.

1. What is a garden? What kinds of gardens can you grow?
2. What is a rose? What does the rose symbolize?
3. What other flowers can you name? Do you think they are as popular as the rose?
4. When you think of a garden, especially a flower garden, what sensory adjectives immediately come to mind?

Now read the paragraph.

EXAMPLE PARAGRAPH

My Mother's Special Garden

My father <u>constantly</u> <u>teased</u> my mother about the amount of time she spent in her beautiful rose garden. He told her that she treated the garden as if it were a human being. However, Mom <u>ignored</u> his teasing and got up very early every morning to take care of her special plants. She ripped out any <u>weeds</u> that threatened her delicate beauties. She also <u>trimmed</u> the old flowers to make room for their bright replacements. Any unwanted <u>pests</u> were quickly killed. When she was finished, she always returned from the garden with a wonderful smile and an armful of <u>fragrant</u> flowers for us all to enjoy.

constantly: always

teased: playfully made fun of someone or something

ignored: did not pay attention to someone or something

weeds: useless plants

trimmed: cut

pests: bugs

fragrant: pleasant smelling

1. What does this paragraph describe?

   _____

   _____

2. Can any sentences be deleted without changing the paragraph's meaning? If yes, which ones, and why? If no, why not?

   _____

   _____

3. The writer's mother treated the roses as if they were human beings. Find two example sentences from the paragraph that show how she protected her roses.

   a. _____

   _____

   b. _____

   _____

LANGUAGE FOCUS: Adjectives

Adjectives are important in a descriptive paragraph. They are like spices—they add flavor to your writing. Compare these two sentences. The underlined words in the second sentence are adjectives.

> The bride walked down the aisle to meet her groom.

> The <u>tall, graceful</u> bride in her <u>white</u> dress walked down the <u>long</u> aisle to meet her <u>proud</u> groom.

Which sentence is more descriptive? The second sentence gives you more sensory information—in this case, the sense of sight. The writer gives a more detailed impression in the second sentence.

What Is an Adjective?

An *adjective* is a part of speech that describes a noun. An adjective usually answers the question: *Which one? What kind? How many?* or *How much?*

Which one?	*this, that, these, those*
What kind?	*big, old, yellow, crumpled*
How many?	*some, few, many, two*
How much?	*enough, bountiful, less, more*

WRITER'S NOTE: Use Adjectives in the Correct Place

It is important to remember that in English an adjective never follows the noun it modifies or describes. Generally, adjectives come before the nouns they modify. In these examples the adjectives are underlined and the nouns are in italics.

> <u>Angry</u> *customers* have complained about <u>poor</u> *service* in the <u>new</u> *restaurant*.

> <u>Blue</u> *skies* ensured that <u>bronzed</u> <u>sun</u> *worshipers* could improve their <u>golden</u> *tans*.

When you proofread your rough draft, circle all of the adjectives and draw a line to the nouns they modify. This will help you notice misplaced adjectives.

> *Incorrect:*   The samovar's shiny sides are decorated with beautiful swirls <u>red</u>.

> *Correct:*   The samovar's shiny sides are decorated with beautiful <u>red</u> swirls.

Adjectives sometimes appear after a linking verb. Advanced learners may want to read the following Grammar Note for a more detailed explanation.

Grammar Note for Advanced Students

When an adjective occurs after a linking verb, it is called a *predicate adjective*. The predicate adjective's job is to modify the subject and complete the meaning of the linking verb. The predicate adjective must *immediately* follow the linking verb.

Some common linking verbs are:

be	become	seem	feel	taste
sound	appear	remain	keep	look

Examples: The <u>teacher</u> is *intelligent* and *kind*.

The <u>soup</u> tastes *good*.

<u>Mr. Cioffi</u> feels *ill*.

The <u>decorations</u> at the dance looked *horrid*!

Activity 4   **Correcting Adjectives**

Read each sentence. Are the adjectives placed correctly? If the sentence is correct, put a C on the line. If you find an adjective error, circle the adjective and draw an arrow to its correct location in the sentence. An example has been done for you.

Example:

_____ John's puppy chewed on his shoes (new.)

1. _____ A yellow piece of paper is on the floor.

2. _____ The teacher wrote our assignment on the blackboard old.

3. _____ My best friend wrote a letter long.

4. _____ The five black dogs chased the police car.

5. _____ Colorado is a place great to go skiing when it is cold.

6. _____ My neighbor found a large wallet filled with new one dollar bills.

7. _____ The gourmet chef created a delicious, nutritious meal.

8. _____ The antique clock on the rough stucco wall of the busy railway station was broken.

9. _____ Egyptian pyramids are an example excellent of ancient architecture.

10. _____ The ducks swimming in the tiny pond had feathers deep green.

Activity 5 | **Adding Adjectives**

Read each sentence. Write adjectives in the blanks to create a more visual description. You may write more than one adjective in a blank. Write your new sentence in the space provided. An example has been done for you.

Example:

The __tired__ teacher walked into the __noisy__ room.

_The tired teacher walked into the noisy room._____

1. The _____ couple watched a _____ sunset.

_____

2. My _____ dog is a _____ pet.

_____

3. The _____ samovar sat on an _____ table.

_____

4. That _____ dog scared my _____ sister.

_____

5. The _____ car raced down the _____ road.

_____

6. My _____ feet ached from walking on the _____ sidewalk.

_____

7. Barbara wore a _____ dress to the _____ party last night.

_____

8. The _____ cow ate _____ grass in the _____ field.

_____

9. A _____ boy sat on the _____ ground and played with some _____ toys.

_____

10. I called my _____ friend yesterday and told her that her _____ cat had run away.

_____

WRITER'S NOTE: Use a Bilingual Dictionary

Most English learners own a bilingual dictionary. A bilingual dictionary is divided into two parts. One part lists words in English with their foreign equivalent(s), and the other part lists a word in a foreign language with its English equivalent(s).

Check the Meanings

A bilingual dictionary is especially helpful when you are first learning English. However, be careful when you use this kind of dictionary. It is easy to choose the wrong word listed in the entry. Always double-check the meaning of the word you choose by checking its equivalent in the other section of your dictionary. This will help make sure that you choose the appropriate word.

Practice with a Word

Practice double-checking meanings by looking up the English word *nice* in your bilingual dictionary. How many meanings are listed? Think of two words that mean *nice* in your language. Look them up in the other part of the dictionary. Was there a change in meaning? Were you surprised by what you found?

LANGUAGE FOCUS: Denotation and Connotation

When you write, it is important to use words that have the precise meaning that you want. Sometimes words have more than one meaning. The *denotation* of a word is its actual, or dictionary, meaning. The *connotation* of a word is its emotional meaning, or the meaning beyond the basic definition. Many words can cause an emotional reaction, either good or bad, in the reader. If you choose a word with the incorrect connotation, you may give your reader the wrong idea.

The <u>thrifty</u> old man saved all his money for his retirement.

The <u>stingy</u> old man saved all his money for his retirement.

Look up *thrifty* and *stingy* in your dictionary. The denotative meanings for these words are similar—they both describe someone who is careful with money. However, there is a big difference in their connotative meanings. The *thrifty* person is wise and economical with money, but the *stingy* person is greedy and does not want to spend or share money.

Words that leave a good emotional impression have a positive connotation. Words that leave a bad emotional impression have a negative connotation. Not all words have a separate connotative meaning. Always check both meanings of new words.

Activity 6   Positive and Negative Connotations of Adjectives

Think of adjectives that describe the nouns listed below. In the first blank, write an adjective that has a positive connotation. In the second blank, write an adjective that has a negative connotation.

Noun	Positive Connotation	Negative Connotation
1. cheese	creamy	rancid
2. rock		
3. painting		
4. laughter		
5. flavor		
6. smell		
7. music		
8. texture		

| **Activity 7** | **Recognizing Adjectives in Paragraphs** |

Below are two descriptive paragraphs about the same topic. Read the paragraphs and underline the adjectives. There are fourteen adjectives in Paragraph 57 and twelve adjectives in Paragraph 58. The first adjective has been underlined for you in both paragraphs.

Paragraph 57

EXAMPLE PARAGRAPH

The Blue River is an <u>important</u> part of the forest, and the quality of the river shapes the environment around it. The fresh, clear water is home to a wide variety of fish and plants. Colorful trout compete with perch for the abundant supply of insects near this beautiful river. The tall shade trees that line the banks are green and healthy. Wild deer come to drink the sweet water and rest in the shadows cast on the grassy banks of the river.

Paragraph 58

EXAMPLE PARAGRAPH

The Blue River is an <u>important</u> part of the forest, and the quality of the river shapes the environment around it. The sluggish brown water contains few fish or plants. Scrawny trout struggle with perch to catch the limited number of insects that live near this dirty river. The old trees near the river are gray and dying. They do not provide protection for the wild animals that come to drink from the polluted river.

1. Briefly, what is being described in each paragraph?

   Paragraph 57 _____

   Paragraph 58 _____

2. What is your impression of the topic in Paragraph 57? What words helped you form this opinion?

   _____

   _____

   _____

   _____

3. What is your impression of the topic in Paragraph 58? What words helped you form this opinion?

   _____

   _____

   _____

   _____

4. Can you find an adjective in one paragraph that has the opposite meaning of an adjective in the other paragraph? For example, we can say that *clear* in Paragraph 57 is opposite in meaning to *brown* in Paragraph 58. Can you find other examples?

   _____

   _____

   _____

   _____

   _____

Activity 8   **Changing Meaning with Connotation**

The paragraph below describes a man walking into a room. Many of the adjectives have been deleted. Fill in each blank with an adjective and create your own paragraph.

The _____ man entered the _____ room. He had

_____ , _____ hair. He wore a _____ suit with

_____ shoes. The man was very _____ . Everyone in the room

was _____ when they saw him. He was such a(n) _____ man!

They couldn't believe that he was in the room with them.

Next, rewrite your paragraph in the space below. Be sure to indent. Then switch books with a partner and compare paragraphs. What impression do you have of the man in your partner's paragraph? Is it positive or negative? Add an original title.

Paragraph 59

_____

_____

_____

_____

_____

_____

Activity 9　　**Original Writing Practice**

Write a paragraph that describes something. Your goal is to give the reader an impression of what you are describing. Follow these guidelines:

- Choose a topic.
- Brainstorm some sensory adjectives (sight, sound, smell, taste, touch).
- Write a topic sentence with controlling ideas.
- Write supporting sentences that relate to the topic.
- Make sure the adjectives mean precisely what you want them to mean—check both the denotation and the connotation.
- Make sure your concluding sentence restates the topic.

If you need help, study the example descriptive paragraphs in this unit. Be sure to refer to the seven steps in the writing process in Appendix 1 on pages 160–168.

Activity 10 Peer Editing

Work with a partner and exchange paragraphs from Activity 9. Then use Peer Editing Sheet 8 on page 205 to help you comment on your partner's paper. Remember that it is important to offer positive comments that will help the writer.

Activity 11 Additional Writing Assignments

Here are some ideas for descriptive paragraphs. When you write, follow the guidelines in Activity 9.

1. Describe a national monument that is important to you. What does it look like? What feelings does the monument inspire in you?

2. Describe a family tradition. When do you follow the tradition? Why is the tradition important to you and your family?

3. Describe your favorite or least favorite meal. Be sure to tell how the food tastes, smells, and looks.

4. Describe something that makes you happy, sad, nervous, or afraid.

5. Describe a person you know. What is this person like? What are some characteristics? Make sure that the description would allow your reader to identify the person in a crowd.

Unit 9

Opinion Paragraphs

GOAL: To learn how to write an opinion paragraph

LANGUAGE FOCUS: Word forms

What do you think of this book? What's your opinion of the weather in your area? Everyone has an opinion about something.

WHAT IS AN OPINION PARAGRAPH?

An opinion paragraph expresses the writer's opinion. A good writer will include not only opinions, but also facts to support his or her opinions. For example, if a writer says "Smoking should not be allowed anywhere," the writer must give reasons for this opinion. One reason could be a fact, such as "Thirty thousand people died in the United States and Canada last year because of lung cancer—a known result of smoking." This fact supports the writer's opinion.

> An opinion paragraph
>
> - gives the writer's opinions about a topic
> - interprets or explains facts
> - is often about a controversial issue
> - makes the reader think
> - considers both sides of an argument

WORKING WITH OPINIONS

It helps to know how you feel about a topic when you read an opinion paragraph. Sometimes the writer may try to persuade you to agree with her or him.

Activity 1   Example Opinion Paragraphs

Read and study these example paragraphs. Answer the questions.

Paragraph 60

This paragraph is about assisted suicide, a controversial topic that many people are discussing nowadays.

Before you read, discuss these questions with your classmates.

1. Do you believe that terminally ill people have the right to end their lives?
2. Do you think that there should be laws to stop people from killing themselves if they are in pain? Why or why not?

Now read the paragraph.

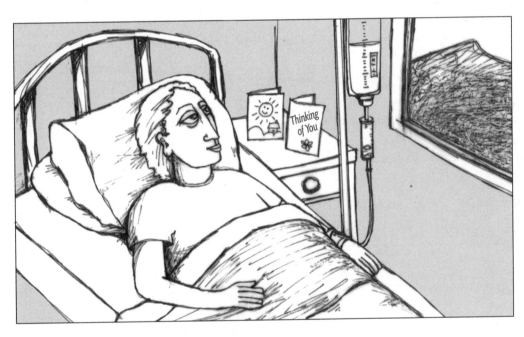

Dying with <u>Dignity</u>

EXAMPLE PARAGRAPH

Studies show that there has been an increase in the number of people who support "medicide," which happens when people with <u>terminal diseases</u> choose to end their lives <u>rather than</u> continue living. One common argument for this growing support is that people should not be forced to continue living if they are in <u>severe</u> pain and cannot live with this <u>constant</u> pain. A second reason is that staying in the hospital for a long time often causes a financial <u>burden</u> on the family. Terminally ill people often worry about the hardship that this will cause their families. Finally, people who are dying sometimes lose hope. Even if they are alive, they can often only lie in bed, and for some people, this is not "life." While many people believe that medicide is an "unnatural way to die" and should remain illegal, sick people should certainly have the right to end their lives if they want.

dignity: pride

terminal diseases: diseases that
   will kill the person

rather than: instead of

severe: serious; intense

constant: continuous, nonstop

burden: something that is difficult
   to bear

1. What is the topic sentence? _____

   _____

2. In your own words, what is "medicide"? (Do not look back at the paragraph.)

   _____

3. List three reasons that people choose medicide.

   a. _____

   b. _____

   c. _____

4. Part of one sentence does not express the author's opinion. Write that partial sentence here:

   _____

5. What is the author's opinion about medicide? _____

   _____

6. What is your reaction to this paragraph? Do you agree or disagree with the author's opinion? Why
   or why not?

   _____

   _____

Paragraph 61

   This paragraph is less serious than Paragraph 60. The subject deals with the question, "Which is better, Coke or Pepsi?"

Before you read, discuss these questions with your classmates.

1. Do you like the taste of Coke? Do you like the taste of Pepsi? Do you have a preference?

2. Do you know what the ingredients in Coke and Pepsi are?

3. Coca-Cola and Pepsi are known all over the world. Why do you think these products are so popular?

Read the following paragraph and see how the writer feels about Coke and Pepsi.

EXAMPLE PARAGRAPH

Always Coca-Cola

<u>No matter</u> how much money Pepsi spends on advertising, Coke will always be better in my opinion. Some people say that the two soft drinks are the same, but I think Coke is much better. First of all, it's not as sweet as Pepsi. It has just the right amount of <u>carbonation</u>, or fizz. In addition, the <u>packaging</u> of the product is unique yet simple. Even if Michael Jackson goes on television and tries to convince me about the greatness of Pepsi, it won't change my mind. For me, it's "always Coca-Cola."

no matter: it doesn't matter or make a difference

carbonation: the bubbly gas in a soft drink

packaging: the way a product looks on the outside

1. What is the topic sentence? _____

_____

2. What phrases from the paragraph show the reader that the writer is giving an opinion and not fact?

_____

_____

3. Do you agree with the observations that the writer makes? Why or why not?

_____

_____

4. Can you think of two other topics that could be compared in a similar way?

_____

_____

Paragraph 62

This paragraph deals with a current controversial issue—school uniforms.

Before you read, discuss these questions with your classmates.

    1. Have you ever worn a school uniform?

    2. Do you think wearing uniforms is a good idea or a bad idea?

    3. What is the best type of uniform for female students? For male students?

Read how the writer feels about this topic.

EXAMPLE PARAGRAPH

School Uniforms Should Receive an A+

    School uniforms should be <u>mandatory</u> for all students for a number of reasons. First, they make everyone equal. In this way, the "rich" kids are on the same level as the poor ones. In addition, getting ready for school can be much faster and easier. Many kids waste time choosing what to wear to school, and they are often unhappy with their final choices. Most important, some <u>studies</u> show that school uniforms make students <u>perform</u> better. Many people might say that uniforms take away from personal freedom, but I believe the benefits are stronger than the <u>drawbacks</u>.

mandatory: obligatory; that must be done

studies: research reports

perform: produce work

drawbacks: disadvantages

    1. What is the author's opinion about school uniforms?

_____

_____

    2. The author gives three reasons to support his opinion. Write them here.

_____

_____

_____

    3. The paragraph states that some people don't agree with school uniforms. What is their main reason?

_____

_____

WRITER'S NOTE: Include an Opposing Opinion

In a good opinion paragraph, the writer

- states an opinion about a topic.

- provides supporting sentences with factual information.

- briefly mentions one opposing point of view. This is called the *counterargument*.

- refutes the counterargument in one or two sentences.

- finishes the paragraph with a concluding sentence that restates the topic sentence and/or offers a solution.

Remember: Most of your supporting sentences will agree with your opinion of the topic. However, it is a good idea to include one opposing point in the paragraph.

Activity 2	Recognizing Good Topic Sentences for Opinion Paragraphs

Read the following sentences. Which ones are good topic sentences for opinion paragraphs? Put a check (✓) next to those sentences.

1. _____ A hospital volunteer usually has many duties.

2. _____ Soccer is a much more interesting game to play and watch than golf.

3. _____ The largest and best-known city in all of France is Paris.

4. _____ Eating a vegetarian diet is the best way to stay healthy.

5. _____ Walt Disney World is the best place for a vacation.

6. _____ The U.S. government uses a system of checks and balances.

7. _____ The Nile River splits into the White Nile and Blue Nile in Sudan.

8. _____ Security alarms are the most effective way to protect homes from burglaries.

FACTS AND OPINIONS

If you choose helpful supporting facts, your opinion paragraph will be stronger. You might even convince readers to agree with you.

Activity 3	Fact versus Opinion

Reread Paragraph 60 about medicide. It contains some information that is factual and some that is the writer's opinion. Find two examples of each in the paragraph and write them on the lines below.

Fact

1. _____

_____

2. _____

_____

Opinion

1. _____

_____

2. _____

_____

LANGUAGE FOCUS: Word Forms

Many English words have different forms, for different parts of speech—noun, verb, adjective, or adverb. In this exercise you will identify word forms. Always check your writing for the correct word forms.

First, study these parts of speech.

A noun names a person or thing.	*growth, agony, illness*
A verb shows action or being.	*desire, equalize*
An adjective describes or modifies a noun.	*financial, unique*
An adverb modifies a verb, adjective, or other adverb.	*sweetly, illegally*

Now complete the chart. Put the word forms in the correct columns. (Some words will not have all four forms.) Use a dictionary if necessary. The first one has been done for you.

	Noun	**Verb**	**Adjective**	**Adverb**
increasingly	increase	increase	increasing	increasingly
increase				
increasing				
increase				
finance				
financially				
finance				
financial				
ill				
illness				
illegality				
illegal				
illegally				
desire				
desirable				
desire				
desirably				

	Noun	Verb	Adjective	Adverb
sweetly	_____	_____	_____	_____
sweetness				
sweet				
sweeten				
simplicity	_____	_____	_____	_____
simply				
simple				
simplify				
equality	_____	_____	_____	_____
equal				
equalize				
equally				
benefit	_____	_____	_____	_____
beneficial				
beneficially				
benefit				
freedom	_____	_____	_____	_____
freely				
free				
free				

Activity 4 — Correcting Word Forms

Some of these sentences contain word form errors. Read each sentence. If the sentence is correct, write C on the line. If it contains an error, write X on the line and correct the word form error.

1. _____ Many people didn't belief the world was round until after Christopher Columbus's voyages.

2. _____ She parked her car illegally and got a $30 ticket.

3. _____ Taking multi-vitamins can be benefit to your health.

4. _____ Students in this classroom are allowed to speak freedom.

5. _____ During civil rights demonstrations, protesters fought for equality.

6. _____ Babies often speak using simply words and phrases.

7. _____ My sister is a very sweetly girl.

8. _____ Mathematicians must use their logical to solve difficult problems.

9. _____ Taxpayers don't want the government to increasing taxes.

10. _____ Mary and Bob's financial situation has improved this year.

Activity 5 — Sequencing Sentences in a Paragraph

The following sentences make up a paragraph. Read the sentences. Then number them from 1 to 6 to indicate the correct order. Put an O or an F on the line after the sentences to indicate whether the sentences contain fact (F) or opinion (O).

a. _____ The damage of these rays may not be seen immediately in children, but

adults who spent a lot of time in the sun when they were children have

a much higher chance of developing skin cancer than adults who did

not spend time in the sun. _____

b. _____ Too much time in the sun can cause severe skin damage, especially in

young children. _____

c. _____ This disease, which can be deadly if it is not treated quickly, is a direct

result of the sun's harmful ultraviolet rays. _____

d. _____ In conclusion, the information in this paragraph is enough evidence to

persuade parents not to let their children play outside in the sun. _____

e. _____ Although many people enjoy playing in the sun, parents should limit the

number of hours that children play outside. _____

f. _____ The most serious example of this is skin cancer. _____

Activity 6   **Copying a Paragraph**

*Now copy the sentences from Activity 5 in the best order to create a good opinion paragraph.
Add a title of your choice.*

Paragraph 63

_____

_____

_____

_____

_____

_____

_____

_____

CHOOSING A TOPIC FOR AN OPINION PARAGRAPH

In Unit 2 you learned about developing ideas for writing paragraphs. This work includes talking about topics and brainstorming. One good source for topics for opinion paragraphs is the newspaper. Most front-page stories in newspapers can become good opinion topics. The editorial section may also help you with ideas.

Two kinds of brainstorming work well for opinion paragraphs. One kind is to brainstorm using the clusters that you did in Unit 2. This will help you think of ideas and supporting information for a topic. It will also help you eliminate unnecessary or unrelated ideas. A second kind of brainstorming is to make two columns about your topic. On one side list the negative ideas about the topic, and on the other side list the positive ideas.

Here is an example of how to set up a negative-positive brainstorm design.

TOPIC: _____

Negative points   **Positive points**

Remember: Whichever argument organization you choose, include at least one sentence that disagrees with your point of view. If you look at the sample paragraphs in this unit, you will find a sentence in each one that goes against the main opinion of the writer. However, the writer states this contrasting point of view and gives facts to refute the idea.

Activity 7 — Original Writing Practice

Develop a paragraph about a strong opinion that you have. Include facts to support your opinion. Follow these guidelines:

- Choose a topic.
- Brainstorm your opinions. If you want, use the newspaper for ideas.
- Write a topic sentence with controlling ideas.
- Write supporting sentences with facts that support your opinions.
- Check for incorrect word forms.

If you need help, study the example opinion paragraphs in this unit. Be sure to refer to the seven steps in the writing process in Appendix 1 on pages 160–168.

Activity 8 — Peer Editing

Work with a partner and exchange paragraphs from Activity 7. Then use Peer Editing Sheet 9 on page 207 to help you comment on your partner's paper. Remember to offer positive comments that will help the writer.

Activity 9 — Additional Writing Assignments

Here are some ideas for opinion paragraphs. When you write, follow the guidelines in Activity 7.

1. Give your opinion about a famous person. Is he or she worthy of this fame? Why or why not?

2. How do you feel about capital punishment? Do you agree or disagree with this method of punishing criminals? Explain your opinions.

3. Should women be allowed in combat positions in the military? Why or why not?

4. When is a person considered an adult?

5. Which do you prefer, classical music or pop music? Why is one better than the other?

Unit 10

Narrative Paragraphs

GOAL: To learn how to write a narrative paragraph

LANGUAGE FOCUS: Consistency in verb tense

Have you read a good story lately? What did you like about it? Readers enjoy a good story when it is told well. When you write a narrative paragraph, you tell a story. The information in this unit will help you write a good narrative paragraph.

WHAT IS A NARRATIVE PARAGRAPH?

The narrative paragraph can be fun to write because you tell a story or relate an event. Narratives have a beginning, a middle, and an end. Any time you go to a movie or read a fiction book, you are looking at a narrative. Narrative paragraphs often describe events from the writer's life.

> A narrative paragraph
>
> - tells a story
> - gives background information in the opening sentence(s)
> - has a beginning, a middle, and an end
> - entertains and informs

WRITER'S NOTE: Including Background Information

The topic sentence of a narrative paragraph—usually the first sentence—gives background information about the action that is going to happen in the story. The backround sentence is not usually the beginning of the story—it sets up the story.

Beginning, Middle, and End

Every narrative paragraph has a beginning, a middle, and an end. Read this example and study the questions and answers.

Paragraph 64

EXAMPLE PARAGRAPH

Background of story (*topic sentence*)	I never thought I could do it, but I finally conquered my fear of public speaking.
Beginning of story	My English teacher gave the assignment (to speak for three minutes in front of my class) at the beginning of the semester, and I worried about it for two months. I have always been afraid of making a speech in public. I wrote all of my ideas on note cards. I practiced my speech with my notes in front of a mirror, in front of my dog, and in front of my husband. Would I be able to make my speech in front of my class?
Middle of story	When the day of my speech came, I was ready. As I reached the podium, I looked at my audience and smiled. Then I looked down at my note cards. At that moment, I realized that I had the wrong information. These were the notes for my biology test, not the information about my speech! I closed my eyes and took a deep breath. Suddenly, I began the speech. To my surprise, the words flowed from my mouth.
End of story	Three minutes later, it was over. Everyone applauded my speech that day, and I left the podium feeling like a winner.

The first sentence in the paragraph—the topic sentence—gives background information about the story. The writer introduces the characters and prepares readers for the action that will come. This sentence is the beginning of the paragraph, but it is *not* usually the beginning of the story.

1. The main character in this paragraph is *I*. What will the story be about?

   The story will probably be about what the writer did or what happened that made her no longer

   afraid of public speaking.

The main action begins after the topic sentence. Not all narratives contain action. They may be about a problem or a conflict.

2. What is the beginning of the main action or problem in this narrative paragraph?

The writer has to make a speech in front of the class, and she is afraid of public speaking. To

help overcome her fear, the writer practiced her speech with notes in three different situations.

After the beginning part, you will find the middle part of the story. This is where the main action or problem occurs.

3. What was the main action or problem? What happened?

The main action is the speech. When the writer stood in front of the class, she discovered

that she had biology notes instead of speech notes.

The end of the story gives the final action or result. If there is a problem or conflict in the story, the solution is presented here.

4. Does the story have a happy or a sad ending? Does the author learn anything from this experience?

The story has a happy ending. Because the writer practiced the speech so many times, she

remembered it without her notes. The writer learned that she has the ability to make a speech

in front of a group.

Activity 1   **Analyzing Example Narrative Paragraphs**

Read and study these example paragraphs. Answer the questions.

Paragraph 65

This paragraph is a personal story about a time when the writer was scared.

Before you read the paragraph, discuss these questions with your classmates.

1. Have you ever felt really scared? Describe the situation.
2. What was going on around you during the scary event? Give some sensory adjectives that describe the surroundings.
3. How did the situation end?

Now read the paragraph.

EXAMPLE PARAGRAPH

My Macy's Nightmare

I'll never forget the first time I got lost in New York City. I was traveling with my parents during summer vacation. We were in Macy's department store, and I was so excited to see such a huge place. Suddenly, I turned around to ask my mom something, but she was gone! I began crying and screaming <u>at the top of my lungs</u>. A salesclerk came up to me and asked if I was okay. She got on the public address (P.A.) system and <u>notified</u> the customers that a little boy with blue jeans and a red cap was lost. Two minutes later my mom and dad came running toward me. We all cried and hugged each other. I'll never forget that day as long as I live.

at the top of my lungs: very loud   **notified:** gave information

1. What is the topic sentence of this paragraph? _____

   _____

2. Where does the story happen? _____

3. How old do you think the boy was? _____

4. What is the beginning of the story? (Circle one.)

   a. He was in a large New York department store.   b. He got separated from his parents.

5. What is the middle of the story? (Circle one.)

   a. He screamed and cried.   b. He got separated from his parents.

6. What is the end of the story? (Circle one.)

   a. His parents found him.   b. The size of the store excited him.

7. What is the writer's purpose for writing this paragraph? _____

   _____

Paragraph 66

This paragraph deals with an embarrassing moment in the writer's life.

Before you read the paragraph, discuss these questions with your classmates.

1. What was the most embarrassing moment in your life? What happened? What was the result?

2. Imagine that you are a waiter or waitress in a restaurant. What is the most embarrassing thing that could happen to you in this job?

Now read the paragraph.

EXAMPLE PARAGRAPH

Friday Night <u>Fiasco</u>

My most embarrassing moment happened when I was working in a Mexican restaurant. I was a <u>hostess</u> working on a busy Friday night. As usual, I was wearing a blouse and a long Mexican skirt. While I was taking some menus to a table, one of the waiters <u>accidentally</u> stepped on the hem of my skirt. I didn't even feel it fall off, and I walked through the whole dining room in my slip. Almost every customer in the restaurant saw me without my skirt on!

fiasco: complete failure

hostess: the person who takes you to your table in a restaurant

accidentally: not intentionally or on purpose

1. What is the topic sentence? _____

_____

2. Why was the writer embarrassed? _____

_____

_____

3. What is the beginning of the story? (Circle one.)

    a. She was embarrassed.   b. She was working in a restaurant.

4. What is the middle of the story? (Circle one.)

    a. Her skirt fell off.   b. She was working in a restaurant.

5. What is the end of the story? (Circle one choice.)

    a. She was embarrassed because   b. She quit her job.
       the customers saw her without
       a skirt.

6. What's the writer's purpose for writing this story? _____

_____

Paragraph 67

    This example narrative paragraph tells about a time in a boy's life when he was unhappy. He learned an important lesson from his unhappiness.

Before you read the paragraph, discuss these questions with your classmates.

1. Think of your best friend. How long have you been best friends?
2. What are the most important qualities in a friend?
3. Have you ever moved away and had to make new friends? Describe the situation. Was it easy? If not, how did you overcome this situation?

Now read the paragraph.

A Lesson in Friendship

    I learned the hard way how to make friends in a new school. At my old school in New Jersey, I was on the football and track team, so I was very popular and had lots of friends. Then, when I was sixteen years old, my parents decided to move to Florida. Going to a new school was not easy for me. The first few days in my new school were extremely hard. All the students dressed <u>casually</u> in shorts and T-shirts instead of a school uniform. Some kids tried to be nice to me, but I didn't want to talk to them. They looked and acted <u>funny</u>! After a few weeks, I realized that no one even tried to talk to me anymore. I began to feel lonely. Two months passed before I <u>swallowed my pride</u> and got the courage to talk to a few classmates. Finally, I realized that they were normal people, just like me. I began to develop some <u>relationships</u>. I learned a <u>valuable</u> lesson about making friends that year.

EXAMPLE PARAGRAPH

casually: informally

funny: strange

swallowed my pride: put self-respect
   aside and accepted the situation

relationships: friendships

valuable: important

1. What is the general topic of this paragraph? _____

_____

2. What is the topic sentence? _____

_____

3. What is the beginning of the story? Write the sentence(s) here.

_____

_____

_____

4. What is the middle of the story? Write the sentences here.

_____

_____

_____

5. What is the end of the story? Write the sentences here.

_____

_____

_____

6. What lesson did the writer learn from this experience?

_____

_____

WORKING WITH IDEAS FOR NARRATIVE PARAGRAPHS

You can find stories in many places, especially your experiences.

| Activity 2 | Recognizing Topics for Narrative Paragraphs |

Read the following paragraph titles. Put a check (✓) next to the titles that you think would make good narrative paragraphs. Be prepared to explain your choices.

_____ My Best Friend Luke   _____ Natural Disasters

_____ How to Become a Doctor   _____ Dalmatians

_____ The Day I Almost Died   _____ A Wonderful Day in the Mountains

Compare your choices to a classmate's. Are they the same or different? Explain.

| Activity 3 | Sequencing Sentences in a Paragraph |

These sentences form a narrative of a personal experience with death. Read the sentences and number them from 1 to 7 to indicate the best order.

a. _____ At 7:18 the next morning, a severe earthquake measuring 8.1 on the Richter scale hit Mexico City. I was asleep, but the violent movement of my bed from side to side woke me up. Then I could hear the rumble of the building as it was shaking.

b. _____ As I tried to stand up, I could hear the stucco walls of the building cracking. I was on the third floor of a six-story building, and I thought the building was going to collapse. I really believed that I was going to die.

c. _____ I flew to Mexico City on September 17. The first two days were uneventful.

d. _____ My trip to Mexico City in September 1985 was not my first visit there, but this unforgettable trip helped me realize something about life.

e. _____ I visited a few friends and did a little sightseeing. On the evening of the eighteenth, I had a late dinner with some friends that I had not seen in several years. It was a very peaceful evening.

f. _____ In the end, approximately 5,000 people died in this terrible tragedy, but I was lucky enough not to be among them. This unexpected disaster taught me that life can be over at any minute, so it is important for us to live every day as if it is our last.

g. _____ When I looked at my room, I could see that the floor was moving up and down like water in the ocean. Because the doorway is often the strongest part of a house, I tried to stand up in the doorway of the bedroom, but I could not even stand up.

Activity 4   Copying a Paragraph

Now copy the sentences from Activity 3 in the best order for a narrative paragraph. Add a title of your choice.

Paragraph 68

_____

Background   _____

information   _____

(topic sentence)

Beginning of story   _____

_____

_____

_____

_____

Middle of story   _____

_____

_____

_____

End of story   _____

_____

_____

_____

_____

LANGUAGE FOCUS: Verb Tense Consistency

When writers tell a story, they usually use the past tense. Consistency in verb tense means that all the verbs are in the same tense. Be careful not to switch tenses when you write a narrative paragraph.

Example

Read this narrative paragraph.

Paragraph 69

Mihai's Surprise

Mihai <u>knew</u> how difficult it <u>was</u> to get a student visa for the United States. However, he <u>gathered</u> all the important paperwork, including his I-20 document, passport, bank statements, and even a letter from his doctor. On the morning of his interview, he jumped on a bus to the capital. For five long hours he rode in silence, looked out the window at the gray landscape, and wondered about the interview. When he arrived at the embassy, he saw a line of more than one hundred people. He patiently waited until a guard gave him a number to enter the warm building. The faces of the embassy personnel frightened him, except for an older woman who reminded him of his grandmother. She was working at window number 4. He hoped that she would be the one to look at his paperwork. When it was his turn, he looked up quickly. The baby-faced worker at window number 3 was calling him to come up. Mihai stepped up to the window and gave all his documents to the young embassy employee. He glanced at "grandma" and thought his chance was gone. Then he heard her say to another man, "You will not get a visa in a thousand years. Next in line, please." He was shocked. He turned to the embassy worker in front of him and heard him say, "Here you are, sir. Your student visa is valid for one year." Mihai couldn't believe it. The impossible happened. Happily, he took his passport and left the building. One day soon he would write about this experience in English in the United States.

Did you notice that all the verbs are in the past tense? Go back and underline the verbs. The verbs in the first two sentences have been done for you.

| **Activity 5** | **Correcting Verb Tenses** |

Read the following narrative paragraph. Underline all the verbs. Then make corrections so that all the verbs are in the past tense.

Paragraph 70

My First Job

EXAMPLE PARAGRAPH

The happiest day of my life is when I get my first job last year. After college, I try

and try for six months to get work with an advertising firm, but my luck is bad. Finally,

one day while I was eating a sandwich in a downtown coffee shop, my luck will begin to

change. A young woman who was sitting next to me asks if she could read my newspaper.

I say okay, and we start talking. She begins to tell me that she is an executive in a huge

advertising company and is looking for an assistant. I will tell her that I am very interested

in mass communications and study it for four years at the university. She gives me her

business card, and within one week, I am her administrative assistant. It is the best lunch

of my life!

Activity 6	Editing Narrative Paragraphs

Read the teacher's comments and the narrative paragraphs. Match the teacher comments to the corrections needed in the paragraphs. Write the number on the line at the end of the paragraph.

Teacher comments

1. Your first sentence is too specific to be a topic sentence. Who is "her"? Your topic sentence should tell the reader what the paragraph is going to be about.

2. Be careful of the verbs. They jump from the present to the past tense.

3. Your paragraph is excellent! The topic sentence sets up the rest of the paragraph very nicely. You also use good supporting sentences and correct verbs.

4. You did not indent the first line of your paragraph. Be careful with correct paragraph form.

5. This is not a narrative paragraph—it's a descriptive one. Follow directions more carefully.

Paragraph 71

EXAMPLE PARAGRAPH

An Unfortunate Family Dinner

My family and I went to her house almost every Sunday, but this one time her food almost made me sick. I asked her what kind of food it was, but she just said that it was healthy and tasty. I looked around the table and saw that everyone else was eating, even my little brother. Without thinking about it, I put some of the reddish brown food in my mouth. Two seconds later I ran into the bathroom and spit everything out. It was the most terrible stuff I had ever eaten! Later that night my grandmother told me what the food was: fried tripe and cow tongue.

_____ **Teacher comment**

Paragraph 72

EXAMPLE PARAGRAPH

Brandy's Luck

My dog Brandy and I went through some great times and some awful times together. I got her for my sixth birthday, and from that time on Brandy never left my side. She used to wait for me to come home from school, and then we would play all afternoon. She was like a part of the family. One day, however, Brandy almost lost

Get Well Soon, Brandy!

EXAMPLE PARAGRAPH

her life. We were playing in the front yard, and she saw a cat on the other side of the street. She did what any normal dog would do. She started to run across the street. I screamed for her to come back, but she didn't listen. Out of nowhere a car appeared and hit her. The driver of the car was very nice and immediately took Brandy to the neighborhood veterinarian. The vet had to operate on Brandy's leg and put her leg in a cast. When my dog finally returned home, she was almost as good as new. From that day, she never left our front yard again.

_____ **Teacher comment**

Paragraph 73

EXAMPLE PARAGRAPH

My Favorite Place

My bedroom is small but comfortable. The walls are covered with posters and banners of my favorite sports teams. On the left side there is a twin bed that I have had since I was ten years old. Next to the bed is my dresser. It is blue and white with gold knobs. Beside the dresser is my bookshelf, which holds most of my schoolbooks, dictionaries, and Kurt Vonnegut novels. Across from the bookshelf you can see my closet. It's too small to hold all my clothes, so some of my stuff has permanent residence on my chair. The clothes get wrinkled there, but I don't mind. My mom doesn't like it that my room is so messy, so one of these days I'm going to clean it up and make her happy.

_____ **Teacher comment**

Paragraph 74

A Travel Nightmare

When I decided to travel across Europe with a backpack, I didn't think I would meet the local police. My best friend and I were sitting in Frankfurt on a train bound for Paris when the nightmare began. A young man comes to the window of the train and asks me what time the train leaves. It took us only ten seconds to open the window and answer him. When we turned away from the window and sat down in our seats, we noticed that our backpacks were missing. Quickly, we got off the train and went to the police headquarters inside the station. We explained what happened. The police officers didn't look surprised. They say it's a common way of stealing bags. One person stays outside the train and asks a passenger for help or information. While the passenger is talking to this person, someone else comes quietly into the train car and steals bags, purses, or other valuables. The "team players" are so good at it that they can get what they want in less than three seconds. The police officers tell us that there is really nothing we can do, but they suggest that we look through the garbage cans and hope that the robbers took only our money and threw our passports and bags away. We looked and looked, but we never found our bags. The next morning we were not in Paris; we were at our embassy in Frankfurt, waiting for duplicate passports.

_____ **Teacher comment**

Paragraph 75

The Trick That Failed

   Twin brothers Freddie and Felix often played tricks at school. One day they decided to try to cheat on a French exam. Freddie was very good at learning languages and was always the best student in both Spanish and French. Felix, however, excelled in mathematics. He was not interested in languages at all. When Felix discovered that he had to take a standardized exam in French, he asked his brother for help. The day of Felix's test, they met in the boys' restroom during lunch and switched clothes. Freddie went to his brother's French class and took the test for him. Meanwhile, Felix followed Freddie's schedule. After school, the twins laughed about their trick and headed home. As they entered the house, their mother called them into the kitchen. She was furious! She had received a phone call from the school principal. The French teacher found out about the trick! "How did he know?" cried Felix. "Easily," replied his mother. "Everyone at the school knows that one obvious difference between you and your brother is that you are right-handed and Freddie is left-handed. While the French teacher was grading the tests, he noticed that the check marks on the test were made by a left-handed person." Felix and Freddie got into a lot of trouble that day, but they learned a valuable lesson—and they never cheated again.

_____ **Teacher comment**

Activity 7   **Original Writing Practice**

Write a narrative paragraph about an experience that you have had. Follow these guidelines:

- Choose a topic.
- Brainstorm the events in your story.
- Write a topic sentence with controlling ideas.
- Write supporting sentences for the middle of your narrative.
- Check for consistency in past tense verbs.
- Write the end of the story.

If you need help, study the example narrative paragraphs in this unit. Be sure to refer to the seven steps in the writing process in Appendix 1 on pages 160–168.

Activity 8   **Peer Editing**

Work with a partner and exchange paragraphs from Activity 7. Then use Peer Editing Sheet 10 on page 209 to help you comment on your partner's paper. Remember to offer positive comments that will help the writer.

Activity 9   **Additional Writing Assignments**

Here are some ideas for narrative paragraphs. When you write your paragraph, follow the guidelines in Activity 7.

1. Write about the most memorable movie you have seen. Describe what happens in the film.

2. Create a short fable using an animal as the main character. What happens to this animal?

3. Write about how someone you know got out of trouble.

4. Write about an important lesson you learned.

5. Write about the most frightening (or happy or difficult) experience you have ever had.

Unit 11

Paragraphs in an Essay: Putting It All Together

GOALS: To understand how paragraphs and essays are related.

To understand the basic steps in composing an essay.

On page 3 of this book we learned what a paragraph is. We saw that a letter becomes a word, a word becomes a sentence, a sentence becomes a paragraph, and a paragraph becomes an essay.

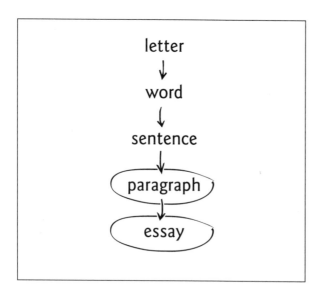

The focus of this unit: how paragraphs form an essay.

In this book, the emphasis is on writing the paragraph. You have studied many different aspects of writing a good paragraph, including the four features of a good paragraph:

158

TOPIC SENTENCE	1. A paragraph has a topic sentence that states the main idea.
Only ONE TOPIC	2. All of the sentences in the paragraph are about one topic.
INDENTED line	3. The first line of a paragraph is indented.
CONCLUDING SENTENCE	4. The last sentence, or concluding sentence, brings the paragraph to a logical conclusion.

The steps in the process of writing a paragraph:

- Developing ideas (brainstorming)
- Creating the topic sentence (focusing the topic)
- Writing supporting sentences (developing the ideas)
- Writing concluding sentences (ending the paragraph)

Now that you have reviewed some facts about paragraphs, it's time to study how paragraphs work together to form an essay. First let's find out what you already know about essays.

Activity 1   What Do You Know about Essays?

Answer these questions. Then work in small groups to compare answers.

1. What do you think an essay is?

   _____

   _____

2. Have you ever written an essay? _____ If yes, what was the topic of the essay?

   _____

   How long was the essay? _____

3. What do you think the differences are between a paragraph and an essay?

   _____

   _____

GETTING TO KNOW ESSAYS

What Is an Essay?

(For more information, see *Great Essays*, pages 4–5.)

An essay is a collection of paragraphs that presents facts, opinions, and ideas on a topic. An essay could be as short as three or four paragraphs or as long as ten or more typed pages that include many paragraphs. Perhaps you have heard of a research paper, which is a special paper that answers a research question. A research paper is actually a kind of essay.

Why Do People Write Essays?

There are many possible reasons.

- As you may know, an essay is a common assignment for students in an English composition class. These students write essays on various topics to practice their writing skills.

- Students also write essays for other classes, such as literature, history, or science. In these classes, the essays are about topics in the subject matter of the course.

- Another occasion for essays is the Test of English as a Foreign Language (TOEFL (R)). For students whose native language is not English, it is often necessary to take this test to be able to enter a college or university. The current TOEFL requires all test takers to write an essay for the Structure and Written Expression (section 2) part of the examination.

- Articles in magazines and other publications are considered essays.

- Some authors collect essays in books about a topic or theme, such as traveling or nature.

How Are Essays and Paragraphs Similar?

Essays are similar to paragraphs in a number of ways.

- They both discuss one topic.

- They both use similar organizational elements to help the reader understand the information.

- Essays have supporting and concluding paragraphs, just as paragraphs have supporting and concluding sentences.

- Both paragraphs and essays have an introduction (or topic sentence), a body (supporting information), and a conclusion.

The following chart shows the main elements that paragraphs and essays have in common.

Comparison of Paragraphs and Essays

	Paragraph	Essay	Function
Introduction	Topic sentence	Hook Thesis statement	Gets readers interested. Gives the main idea.
Body	Supporting sentences	Topic sentences Supporting paragraphs	Organize the main points. Give supporting information.
Conclusion	Concluding sentence	Concluding paragraph	Signals the end of the writing.

How Are Essays and Paragraphs Different?

The main difference between an essay and a paragraph is the length and, therefore, the scope of the information. Remember that the length depends on the topic and on the purpose of the writing. Imagine that your teacher gives you the general topic of university education. You are asked to write a paragraph about something related to university education. A paragraph usually has five to ten sentences, so you must narrow your subject to include the most important information in these few sentences. Your paragraph topic could be the tuition costs at the university.

On the other hand, your teacher might ask you to write an essay about university education. Your essay will need to include several paragraphs about a larger topic, such as a comparison of university and community college education. In general, a paragraph topic is very specific while the essay topic must cover a wider scope.

Activity 2   **Topics for Paragraphs and Essay**

Each pair of sentences is about one topic. Decide which sentence is the topic sentence for a paragraph (P) and which is the thesis statement for an essay (E). (HINT: The thesis statements cover more information.)

1. Topic: Japanese customs

   A. _____ If you travel to Japan, you should first find out about Japanese customs, taboos, and people.

   B. _____ The worst mistake that a foreigner can make with Japanese customs is standing up chopsticks in a bowl of rice.

2. Topic: Education in Taiwan and the United States

    A. _____ One difference between the educational systems in Taiwan and the United States is the role of sports programs in the curriculum.

    B. _____ Because I have studied in both countries, I have seen several areas in which education in Taiwan and education in the United States are different.

3. Topic: Household chores

    A. _____ Ironing clothes is a dreaded household task because it cannot be completed quickly or thoughtlessly.

    B. _____ The three most dreaded household tasks include ironing clothes, washing dishes, and cleaning the bathroom.

4. Topic: School uniforms

    A. _____ Wearing school uniforms is a good choice for public school students for a number of reasons.

    B. _____ Wearing school uniforms would make students' lives much simpler.

5. Topic: Capital punishment

    A. _____ Some people say that the government doesn't have the right to end someone's life, but the following reasons will show why capital punishment is appropriate.

    B. _____ One reason that capital punishment is appropriate is financial: It's cheaper to execute someone than to support him or her in prison.

WHAT DOES AN ESSAY LOOK LIKE?

There are many different kinds of essays just as there are many different kinds of paragraphs. The following example essay is simple, clearly organized, and easy to understand. It was written by a student in an English composition class. This was the assignment: "Many inventions in the past one hundred years have changed people's lives. In your opinion, which invention has been the most important and why? Use specific examples and details in your essay."

As you read the essay, notice the thesis statement that states the main idea of the essay, the topic sentence in each paragraph, and the transition words that help connect ideas.

Essay 1

The Most Important Invention in the Past Century

1   When you woke up today, you turned on the lights, ran the hot water in the shower, put on mass-produced clothing, watched television, drove to work, and spoke on the telephone. Every day we are surrounded by thousands of useful things that were invented only a relatively short time ago. *In fact* we depend on these things for the good quality   ← **Transition**
of life that we have now. **All of these inventions have been very important to**   ← **Thesis**
humans, but the one that has been the most important in improving people's   **Statement**
health over the centuries is the discovery of antibiotics.

2   The Bubonic Plague, which killed millions of Europeans six hundred years ago, was   ← **Topic Sentence**
nothing more than a bacterium. It was spread by rodents and fleas, which were so common during that time. This disease was also called the Black Death because when a person contracted the disease, his or her neck and face would swell up and turn black. Back then, no one was aware that this plague could have easily been treated with penicillin. The Black Plague eventually retreated, but people were still in danger of dying from simple bacteria.

3   Even as recently as one hundred years ago, medical knowledge was much more lim-   ← **Topic Sentence**
ited than it is now. Something as trivial as a simple cut could sometimes result in an amputation or even death if it became infected. Medical professionals knew what was happening; *however*, there was simply no way to stop the infection from spreading or   ← **Transition**
causing more harm. The discovery of penicillin in the early part of the twentieth century changed all of that. Antibiotics finally allowed humans to maintain their good health and continue their lives for many more years.

4   *In fact*, antibiotics are an inexpensive and effective treatment for a number of ail-   ← **Topic Sentence**
ments. When we have an infection nowadays, we don't think about it too much. We   **Transition**
go to the doctor, who will prescribe some kind of medicine. We take this medicine as directed, and *then*, after a few days, we are healthy again. The medicine is probably a   ← **Transition**
form of antibiotics. *In addition*, these antibiotics are painless and fast acting. Without   ← **Transition**
them, countless people would suffer through painful and life-threatening ailments.

5   When people think of the most important invention in the past one hundred years, most people think about electricity, the car, airplanes, or computers. While all of these   ← **Topic Sentence**
are certainly extremely important, the invention of antibiotics promoted good health and longer lives. People tend to take antibiotics and other medicine for granted, but they should not do this. If antibiotics had not been invented in the past century, millions of people would have died much earlier, and human beings would not be able to enjoy the style of life that exists today.

rodent: a small, often disease-carrying animal such as a rat

flea: a small insect that lives on cats and dogs; it jumps very quickly

contract: to get something, such as a disease

trivial: not important

amputation: the removal of an exterior body part, such as a leg or arm

infected: to have disease-producing bacteria (or similar substances) in the body

ailment: a sickness; an illness

An Essay Outline

(For more information, see *Great Essays*, pages 33–36.)

The steps in writing a paragraph are similar to the steps in writing a good essay. After you brainstorm a suitable topic for an essay or paragraph, you think about an introduction, supporting ideas, and a conclusion. For an essay, an important step is to make an outline. Here is an outline of "The Most Important Invention in the Past Century" that you just read. Reread the essay before you read the outline. Then find the outline information in the essay to help you understand its organization.

I. Introduction (paragraph 1)—Many important things have been invented in the past century, but the most important was the discovery of antibiotics.

II. Body (paragraph 2)—Hundreds of years ago, millions of Europeans died from Bubonic Plague.

II. Body (paragraph 3)—Medicine was limited until the invention of penicillin in the early twentieth century.

IV. Body (paragraph 4)—Antibiotics are currently used for a variety of ailments.

V. Conclusion (paragraph 5)—<u>The invention of antibiotics promoted good health and longer lives.</u>

WRITER'S NOTE: Vary Your Vocabulary

Vocabulary is a key part of good writing. The level of vocabulary that you use is an indication of your English proficiency. Better vocabulary often favorably influences the reader's opinion of your writing.

Note that the vocabulary in the outline is not always the same as the vocabulary in the essay. VARIETY is important! In your essays, try to use synonyms, phrases, and sometimes whole sentences to say the same information in a different way. Avoid using the same vocabulary all the time.

The Thesis Statement

(For more information, see *Great Essays*, pages 25–26, 41.)

We learned that the most important part of any paragraph is the topic sentence. The first paragraph of an essay has a similar sentence that is called a thesis statement. It tells the reader what the essay is about. The thesis statement also indicates what the organization of the essay will be. The thesis statement is usually the last sentence in the introduction paragraph. Find and reread the thesis statement in "The Most Important Invention in the Past Century." (Answer: All of these inventions have been very important to humans, but the most important one in improving people's health over the centuries is the discovery of antibiotics.)

Now read these examples of thesis statements:

1. Three things make traveling to Southeast Asia an unforgettable experience.

2. Serving in the military offers not only professional advantages but also personal advantages.

3. Computer literacy is one of the fastest growing needs for young adults.

4. The person I most respect and admire is my grandmother Josephine.

As you can see, the topics for the essays with these thesis statements range from serious subjects to personal stories. The thesis statement that you write will depend on the assignment that your teacher gives you.

Supporting Ideas

(For more information, see *Great Essays*, page 9.)

Essays need supporting ideas just like paragraphs. Writers should have two or three ideas that support the thesis statement. These ideas will eventually become paragraphs. Asking a question about the thesis statement is a good way to come up with material for supporting paragraphs. Remember that it is important to provide specific examples and details.

Here are some questions to ask and ideas to develop about the thesis statements you read above.

1. Three things make traveling to Southeast Asia an unforgettable experience.

   Question: Why is it an unforgettable experience?

   Ideas to develop: the people are very friendly; there are beautiful places to see; the food is exotic.

2. Serving in the military offers not only professional advantages but also personal advantages.

   Question: What are these advantages?

   Ideas to develop: Professional advantages: a full-time job with good benefits, vocational training; Personal advantages: a sense of pride in serving your country, developing maturity

3. Computer literacy is one of the fastest growing needs for young adults.

   Question: Why is the need for computer literacy so important?

   Ideas to develop: Computer literacy is essential for advanced studies (college or university), for the workplace, and for life in general (banking, buying and selling, etc.).

4. The person I most respect and admire is my grandmother Josephine.

   Question: Why do you admire her so much?

   Ideas to develop: she taught me about hard work; she loved me unconditionally; she always gave me excellent advice.

Different Kinds of Essay Organization

Once you write a thesis statement, you can develop your essay in different ways. In the following activity, you will work with some possibilities for essay organization:

Activity 3	Working with Essay Organization

Read the thesis statements. For the last two, write a brief outline that shows how you might organize the essay. Study the first three examples. Note: Essays usually have five to ten paragraphs.

1. Prisoner rehabilitation has succeeded by providing various programs that help inmates function in the real world when they are released.

     I. Introduction (paragraph 1)
     II. Body (paragraph 2): rehabilitation program 1
     III. Body (paragraph 3): rehabilitation program 2
     IV. Body (paragraph 4): rehabilitation program 3
     V. Body (paragraph 5): example of a prison that uses all three of these rehabilitation programs
     VI. Conclusion (paragraph 6)

2. Three things make traveling to Southeast Asia an unforgettable experience.

     I. Introduction (paragraph 1)
     II. Body (paragraph 2): thing 1
     III. Body (paragraph 3): thing 2
     IV. Body (paragraph 4): thing 3
     V. Conclusion (paragraph 5)

3. Serving in the military offers not only professional advantages but also personal advantages.

     I. Introduction (paragraph 1)
     II. Body (paragraph 2): professional advantage 1
     III. Body (paragraph 3): professional advantage 2
     IV. Body (paragraph 4): personal advantage 1
     V. Body (paragraph 5): personal advantage 2
     VI. Body (paragraph 6): comparison of the professional and personal advantages
     VII. Body (paragraph 7): example of a person in the military who benefited from these four advantages
     VIII. Conclusion (paragraph 8)

4. Computer literacy is one of the fastest growing needs for young adults.

_____

_____

_____

_____

_____

5. The person I most respect and admire is my grandmother Josephine.

_____

_____

_____

_____

_____

Activity 4   **Comparing Outlines**

Now work in groups to compare your outlines from Activity 3. Discuss how you would develop the ideas in the essays in numbers 4 and 5, based on your outline.

Activity 5   **Working with a Sample Essay**

Read and study the following essay. Then work with a partner to answer the questions that follow.

Essay 2

The Benefits of Being Bilingual

1   The Vieira family moved to the United States in 1981. At that time, they made a decision. They decided to stop speaking Portuguese at home and only communicate in English. They were, in fact, living in an English speaking country. The Vieira children

are adults now, and from time to time they travel to Portugal to visit old family and friends. There's a problem, however. Mr. and Mrs. Vieira's offspring cannot communicate with their relatives. This particular event happens frequently all over the world. When people immigrate to new lands, many of them begin disregarding not only their cultural traditions but also their native language. This disregard for the native language is a mistake, as there are many benefits to being bilingual.

2   One of the most basic advantages of being bilingual is a purely linguistic one. People who can speak more than one language can communicate with more people around the world. They don't have to rely on another person to automatically know their own language or resort to an interpreter to get their message across. These bilingual people are independent and self-reliant. Their message can be heard and understood without the 'aid' of others' help. In contrast, people who are monolingual must put all their trust in others in order to make communication happen. Bilinguals are masters of their words and ideas.

3   In addition to linguistic advantages, speaking a second language also allows people to experience another culture. Even if these people have never visited another country, bilingualism enhances cultural and social awareness of another group of people. Idiomatic expressions, vocabulary, and even jokes can have a powerful impact on a person's understanding of another culture. For example, a person who speaks American English knows the expression "to put your John Hancock" on something. The basic meaning is to sign something. However, this expression has a much larger historical context. When the American colonists wrote the Declaration of Independence, some were afraid to sign their name because this action put their lives in danger. However, John Hancock was not afraid and wrote his name first on the list and in very big letters so the King would have no trouble seeing it. From this part of American history and culture, we have the modern expression "to put your John Hancock" on a document. Not having a background in American culture and history might limit a person's understanding of this expression.

4   Finally, widespread bilingualism can contribute to global awareness. If everyone in the world spoke a second or third language, the different areas of the world could become more closely entwined and cohesive. Countries could better communicate and perhaps have a better global understanding of others' ideas, values, and behaviors. Being able to speak another country's language makes people more sympathetic to the problems and situations in that country. Conversely, not knowing the language of a potential enemy (country) can only increase miscommunication and suspicion.

5   The benefits of bilingualism are clear. In fact, there is no single disadvantage to speaking more than one language. The real tragedy, however, is not that people do not make the effort to study and learn a second language. It is that people who already have the gift of speaking another tongue let themselves forget it and therefore become a part of the muted majority.

1. How does the essay begin? Circle the best answer.

   a fact   an opinion   a story

2. Reread the concluding paragraph. Circle the word that best describes it.

   suggestion   opinion   prediction

3. Which paragraph discusses the cultural benefits of speaking a second language?

   Circle the best answer.

   Paragraph 1   Paragraph 3   Paragraph 5

4. Which paragraph discusses the global benefits of bilingualism? Circle the best

   answer.

   Paragraph 1   Paragraph 2   Paragraph 4

5. Which paragraph gives the author's opinion about people who lose a language?

   Paragraph 2   Paragraph 3   Paragraph 5

Activity 6   **Working with an Outline**

Reread "The Benefits of Being Bilingual" and complete the outline.

   I. Introduction (paragraph 1)

      A. Hook: Story of Vieira children

      B. Thesis statement: _____

         _____

   II. Body

      A. Paragraph 2 Topic Sentence: _____

         _____

         1. Supporting idea: They can communicate with more people

         2. Supporting idea: They don't need an interpreter

         3. Supporting idea: They are in charge of their own ideas

         4. Supporting idea: Monolingual people cannot speak on their own

B. Paragraph 3 Topic Sentence: Speaking a second language also allows people to experience another culture.

    1. Supporting idea: More cultural and social awareness of another group of people

    2. Supporting idea: Idiomatic expressions, vocabulary, and jokes help people understand a different culture

    3. Supporting idea (example): _____

       _____

C. Paragraph 4 Topic Sentence: _____

   _____

    1. Supporting idea: Countries could become closer

    2. Supporting idea: _____

       _____

    3. Supporting idea: Not knowing an enemy country's language can increase miscommunication.

II. Concluding paragraph (paragraph 5)

A. Restatement of thesis: Bilingualism has only positive effects.

B. Opinion: _____

   _____

PUTTING AN ESSAY TOGETHER

Now that you have learned some of the basics of an essay, it is time to practice writing one. In the following activities, you will work with your classmates to produce an essay.

Activity 7   Brainstorming

Read the following essay topic, then follow the directions.

Topic: **Living in a big city is better than living in a small town.**

1. Form three groups. Each group must brainstorm and come up with as many reasons as possible why living in a large city is better than living in a small town.

   Your group: _____

   _____

   _____

   _____

2. When you have finished brainstorming, write all your ideas on the board. As a class, vote for the three best reasons. These will become the topic sentences for your essay. Each group will be responsible for one of the reasons. Write them here.

   Group 1: _____

   _____

   Group 2: _____

   _____

   Group 3: _____

   _____

3. Choose one of the three reasons. This is your topic sentence. Brainstorm some examples that support your topic sentence.

   _____

   _____

   _____

   _____

4. When you are finished, share the information with the rest of the class. (Fill in the list
   below.)

Group 1 Reason: _____

Example: _____

_____

Group 2 Reason: _____

Example: _____

_____

Group 3 Reason: _____

Example: _____

_____

| **Activity 8** | **Writing an Essay Draft** |

*You are now ready to complete an essay. Read the following partial essay and fill in the blanks
with the information you gathered.*

Essay 3

Advantages of City Life

1 The population of Small Hills is 2,500. Everyone knows everyone else. The mayor of the
city is also the owner of the sporting goods store. There is only one school in Small Hills,
and all the students know each other, from age six to age eighteen. Every weekend, many
residents of Small Hills go to the only restaurant in town, and perhaps after dinner they
go to the only cinema. This routine continues. The population of Los Angeles is approximately 3 million. It is a city that is so culturally diverse that at any given time one can
go to any type of restaurant, watch any type of film, and see countless exhibits and
museums. Which type of life is better? It seems obvious that living in a large city full of
diversity is much better than living in a small and rural community.

2 First, living in a large city is better because _____

_____

_____

_____

_____

_____

3 In addition, city life can _____

_____

_____

_____

_____

EXAMPLE ESSAY

4 Finally, large cities give people the opportunity to _____

_____

_____

_____

_____

_____

5 In conclusion, there are many benefits to living in a large city. While some people might be afraid of existing among such a large and often chaotic group of people, the benefits that a large city can afford its citizens are well worth it. Besides, there is always a place to find tranquillity, even in busy metropolitan areas.

Activity 9 | **Peer Editing**

Work with a partner and exchange essays from Activity 8. Then use Peer Editing Sheet 11 on page 227 to help you comment on your partner's paper. Remember that it is important to offer positive comments that will help the writer.

NEXT STEPS

In this unit we have presented an introduction to writing an essay. We have pointed out the similarities between writing a paragraph and writing an essay. If you understand the components of a paragraph and the steps in the process of writing a paragraph, then writing an essay should be a relatively easy next step for you.

To complete any essay assignment, be sure to follow the steps of the writing process at the back of this book and at the back of *Great Essays*. The most important steps for both paragraphs and essays are (1) choose a good topic, (2) brainstorm ideas, (3) outline/organize ideas, (4) write a rough draft, (5) revise, (6) re-read (or exchange papers with another student for peer review), (7) do a final revision (checking for clarity, language, organization, and cohesion).

The companion book *Great Essays* can now take you further into writing essays. *Great Essays* presents essay writing in more detail and with many more activities and opportunities for writing practice. In learning to write both paragraphs and essays, it is important to write a lot—practice, practice, practice!

TOPICS FOR WRITING

Activity 10   **Essay Writing Practice**

Write an essay about one of the topics in this list.

Narrative Essay:	Tell a story about a time in your life when you were very afraid.
Comparison Essay:	What are the differences between being an entrepreneur and working for a company?
Cause-Effect Essay:	Why do people get divorced?
Argumentative Essay:	Should high schools include physical education in their curriculum or devote their time to teaching only academic subjects?

Part III

Additional Writing Practice

Appendix 1

Understanding the Writing Process: The Seven Steps

This section can be studied at any time during the course. You will want to refer to the seven steps many times as you write your paragraphs.

THE ASSIGNMENT

Imagine that you have been given the following assignment: *Write a definition paragraph about a common item or thing.*

What should you do first? What should you do second, and so on? There are many ways to write, but most good writers follow certain general steps in the writing process.

Look at this list of steps. Which ones do you do? Which ones have you never done?

1. Choosing a topic

2. Brainstorming

3. Rough draft

4. Cleaning up the rough draft

5. Peer editing

6. Revising the draft

7. Final draft

Now you will see how one student went through all the steps to do the assignment. First, read the final paragraph that Susan gave her teacher. Read the teacher's comments as well.

EXAMPLE PARAGRAPH

Gumbo

The dictionary defines gumbo as "a thick soup made in south Louisiana." However, anyone who has tasted this delicious dish knows that this definition is too bland to describe gumbo. It is true that gumbo is a thick soup, but it is much more than that. Gumbo, one of the most popular of all the Cajun dishes, is made with various kinds of seafood or meat mixed with vegetables such as green peppers and onions. For example, seafood gumbo contains shrimp and crab. Other kinds include chicken, sausage, and turkey. Regardless of the ingredients in gumbo, it is invariably served in a bowl over rice.

100/A+   Excellent paragraph!

I enjoyed reading about gumbo. Your paragraph is very well-written. All the sentences revolve around one single subject. I really like the fact that you used so many connectors (however, such as).

Now look at the steps that Susan went through to compose the paper you just read.

STEPS IN THE WRITING PROCESS

STEP 1: Choosing a Topic

Susan chose gumbo as her topic. This is what she wrote about her choice.

EXAMPLE WRITING

When I first saw the assignment, I didn't know what to write about. I didn't think I was going to be able to find a good topic.

First, I tried to think of something that I could define. It couldn't be something that was really simple like television or a car. Everyone already knows what they are. I thought that I should choose something that most people might not know.

I tried to think of general areas like sports, machines, and inventions. However, I chose food as my general area. Everyone likes food.

Then I had to find one kind of food that not everyone knows. For me, that wasn't too difficult. My family is from Louisiana, and the food in Louisiana is special. It is not the usual food that most Americans eat. One of the dishes we eat a lot in Louisiana is gumbo, which is a kind of thick soup. I thought gumbo would be a good topic for a definition paragraph because not many people know it, and it's sort of easy for me to write a definition for this food.

Another reason that gumbo is a good choice for a definition paragraph is that I know a lot about this kind of food. I know how to make it, I know what the ingredients are, and I know what it tastes like. It's much easier to write about something that I know than about something that I don't know about.

After I was sure that gumbo was going to be my topic, I went on to the next step, which is brainstorming.

STEP 2: Brainstorming

The next step for Susan was to brainstorm.

In this step, you write down every idea that pops into your head about your topic. Some of these ideas will be good, and some will be bad—write them all down. The main purpose of brainstorming is to write down as many ideas as you can think of. If one idea looks especially good, you might circle that idea or put a check next to it. If you write down an idea and you know right away that you are not going to use it, you can cross it out.

Look at Susan's brainstorming diagram on the topic of gumbo.

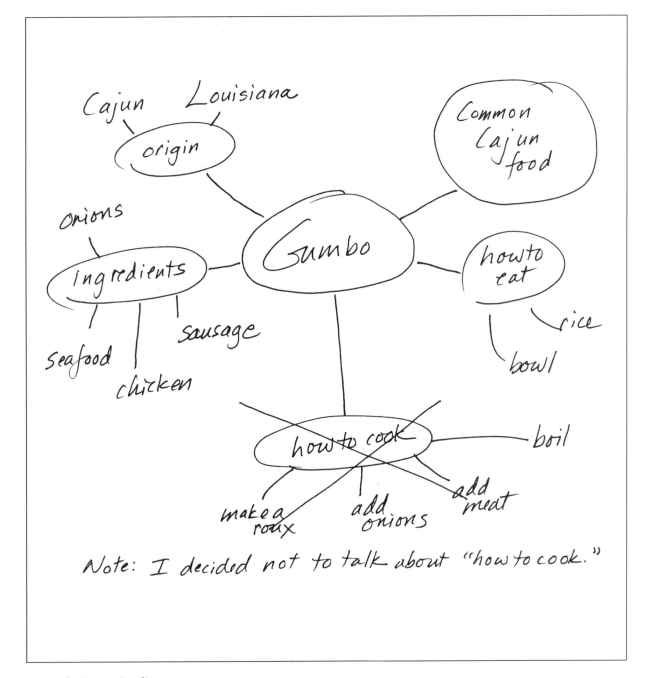

Susan's brainstorming diagram

STEP 3: Writing a Rough Draft

Next, Susan wrote a rough draft. In this step you take information from your brainstorming session and write a rough draft. This first draft may contain many errors, such as misspellings, incomplete ideas, and incorrect punctuation. At this point, don't worry about correcting the errors. The main thing is to put your ideas into sentences.

You may feel that you do not know what you think about the topic yet. In this case, it may be difficult for you to write, but it is important to just write, no matter what comes out. Sometimes writing helps you think, and as soon as you form a new thought, you can write it.

Read Susan's rough draft.

Introduction is weak ??? Use dictionary!

(Rough draft)
Susan Mims

Do you know what gumbo is. It is a seafood soup. However, gumbo is really more than a kind of soup, it is special. ???

Gumbo is one of the most popular of all Cajun dish. (es)

Combine
It is made with various kind(s) of seafood or meet. (meat)
This is mixed with vegetables such as onions. (+ green peppers)

Combine
Seafood Gumbo is made with shrimp and crab.
Also chicken, sausage, and turkey, etc. Regardlss (ok ???)
of what is in gumbo, it is usually served in (a) bowl
over (the) rice.

— Is this correct? Ask teacher!

Susan's rough draft

What do you notice about this rough draft? Here are a few things that a good writer should pay attention to:

- First of all, remember that this is not the final copy. Even native speakers who are good writers usually write more than one draft. You will have a chance to revise the paper and make it better.

- Look at the circles, question marks, and writing in the margin. These are notes that Susan made to herself about what to change, add, or reconsider.

- Remember that the paper will go through the peer editing process later. Another reader will help you make your meaning clear and will look for errors.

STEP 4: Cleaning Up the Rough Draft

In addition to the language errors that writers often make in the first draft, the handwriting is usually not neat. Sometimes it is so messy that only the writer can read it!

After you make notes on your rough draft, put it away for several hours or a few days. You may find it helpful to come back to the paper later when your mind is clear and you are more likely to catch problems. At that time, copy the draft again in a neater hand, or type it on a computer if you have one. If you notice any words or sentences that do not belong, do not be afraid to take them out. At this time you may also want to add ideas that make the paper better.

Now read Susan's cleaned-up rough draft. Compare it to her rough draft on page 163.

The dictionary defines gumbo as "a thick soup made in ∧south Louisiana." However, all the people who have tasted gumbo know that this definition is too simple to describe gumbo. It is true that gumbo is a thick soup, but it's much more than that. Gumbo, one of the most popular Cajun dishes, is made with various kinds of seafood or meat mixed with vegetables such as green peppers and onions. Seafood gumbo is made with shrimp, crab, chicken, sausage, and turkey, etc. Regardless of what is in gumbo, it is usually served in a bowl over rice.

Cleaned-up rough draft

STEP 5: Peer Editing

After Susan finished the cleaned-up copy of the rough draft, she exchanged papers with another student, Jim, in her class. Here is the peer editing sheet that Jim completed about Susan's paragraph. Read the questions and answers.

PEER EDITING SHEET

Writer: _Susan_   Date: _2-14_

Peer editor: _Jim_

1. What is the general topic of the paper? _gumbo_

2. What is the writer's purpose? (in 15 words or less)

   to define gumbo

3. Is the paragraph indented?   (yes)   no   (Circle one.)

4. How many sentences are there? _6_

5. Is the first word of every sentence capitalized?   (yes)   no
   If no, circle the problem on the paper.

6. Does every sentence end with correct punctuation?   (yes)   no
   If no, circle the problem on the paper.

7. Are there any capitalization or punctuation errors?   yes   (no)
   Circle these problems on the paper.

8. Write the topic sentence here:

   The dictionary defines gumbo as "a thick soup made in south Louisiana."

9. Do you think the topic sentence is good for this paragraph? Comments?

   Yes. All of the other sentences are 100% connected to the idea in this sentence.

10. Does the paragraph talk about just one topic?   (yes)   no

   If no, what is the extra topic? _____

   In what sentence is this material? _____

11. Grammar: Does every sentence have a verb?   (yes)   no
   If not, circle the errors on the paper.

12. Grammar: Write any mistakes that you found and the correction.

   error 1: _____ it's—don't use contractions in formal writing _____

   correction: _____ it is _____

   error 2: _____ etc.—Don't use this. _____

   correction: _____ I don't know. You should list all the kinds. _____

   error 3: _____

   correction: _____

13. Did you have any trouble understanding this paragraph?   yes   (no)

   If yes, tell where/why.

   _____

14. Expansion of information: What questions do you have about the content? What other information should be in this paragraph?

   How do you make gumbo? Is it easy to cook? Why do you think people started making gumbo?

15. What is your opinion of the writing of this paragraph?

   It's good, but reread the second sentence. It seems long. Also, don't repeat "gumbo" so much.

   Don't use "is" so much!

16. What is your opinion of the content of this paragraph?

   I like the topic. I think I ate gumbo at a restaurant once.

Thank you for reading this paper and making comments!

In the next step, you will see how Susan used these suggestions and information to revise her paragraph.

STEP 6: Revising the Draft

This step consists of three parts:

1. Reacting to the comments on the peer editing sheet
2. Rereading the paragraph and making changes
3. Rewriting the paragraph one more time

Here is what Susan wrote about the changes she decided to make.

EXAMPLE WRITING

   I decided to rewrite the second sentence. I tried to cut some words. Also, I used "this delicious dish" and other expressions instead of repeating "gumbo" so many times.

   I didn't use all of the suggestions that the peer editor made. I thought that some of his questions were interesting, but the answers were not really part of the purpose of this paragraph, which is to define gumbo.

   I was happy that the peer editor was able to understand all my ideas fully. To me, this means that my writing is good enough.

Now read Susan's revised draft.

○	Gumbo
	The dictionary defines gumbo as "a thick soup made in south Louisiana." However, anyone who has tasted this delicious dish knows that this definition is too bland to describe gumbo. It is true that gumbo is a thick soup, but it is much more than that. Gumbo, one of the most popular of all Cajun dishes, is made with vegetables such as green peppers and onions. For example, seafood gumbo contains shrimp and crab. Other kinds
○	include chicken, sausage, and turkey. Regardless of the ingredients in gumbo, it is ~~usually~~ invariably served in a bowl over rice.

Revised draft

Follow the three directions in this step on your paper.

STEP 7: Proofing the Final Paper

Most of the hard work should be over by now. In this step, the writer pretends to be a brand-new reader who has never seen the paper before. The writer reads the paper to see if the sentences flow smoothly.

Read Susan's final paper again on page 161. Notice that she made a change in vocabulary at this stage.

Of course the very last step is to turn the paper in to your teacher and hope that you get a good grade!

Appendix 2

Capitalization Practice

BASIC CAPITALIZATION RULES

1. Always capitalize <u>the first word of a sentence</u>.

   Today is not Sunday.

   It is not Saturday either.

   Do you know today's date?

2. Always capitalize the word *I* no matter where it is in a sentence.

   John brought the dessert, and I brought some drinks.

   I want some tea.

   The winners of the contest were Ned and I.

3. Capitalize proper nouns—the names of specific people, places, or things.

   Mr. Lee parked his Toyota in front of the Hilton.

   The Statue of Liberty is located on Liberty Island in New York.

   There is a nice statue on that island, isn't there?

4. Titles. If you look at the sample paragraphs in this book, you will notice that each of them begins with a title. In a title, pay attention to which words begin with a capital letter and which words do not.

Gumbo	*Dying with Dignity*	*Always Coca-Cola*
The King and I	*Three Men and a Baby*	*Love at First Sight*

The rules for capitalizing titles are easy.

- Always capitalize the first letter of a title.

- If the title has more than one word, capitalize all the words that have meaning (content words).

- Do not capitalize small (function) words like *a, the, in, with, on, for, to, above, and,* or

CAPITALIZATION PRACTICE

Practice 1   *Circle the words that have capitalization errors. Make the corrections.*

1. the last day to sign up for the trip to miami is this Thursday.

2. does jill live in west bay apartments, too?

3. the flight to new york left late saturday night and arrived early sunday morning.

4. My Sister has two daughters. Their names are rachel and rosalyn.

5. if mercedes cars weren't so expensive, i think i'd buy one.

Practice 2   *Complete these statements. Be sure to use correct capitalization.*

1. USA stands for United _____ of _____ .

2. The seventh month of the year is _____ .

3. _____ is the capital of France.

4. One of the most popular brands of jeans is _____ .

5. President Kennedy's first name was _____ . His wife's first name was

_____ .

6. Much of Europe was destroyed in _____ (1939–45).

7. All over the world you can see the large golden M that belongs to the most popular fast-food

place, _____ .

8. Beijing is the largest city in _____ .

9. The winter months are _____ , _____ , and _____ .

10. The last movie that I saw was _____ .

Practice 3   *Read the following titles. Rewrite them with correct capitalization.*

1. my favorite food   _____

2. living in miami   _____

3. the best restaurant in town   _____

4. mr. smith's new car   _____

5. a new trend in hollywood   _____

6. why i left california   _____

7. my side of the mountain   _____

8. no more room for a friend   _____

Practice 4   *Read the following paragraph. Circle the capitalization errors and make corrections above.*

Paragraph 76

EXAMPLE PARAGRAPH

A visit to Cuba

according to an article in last week's issue of *newsweek*, the prime minister of canada

will visit cuba soon in order to establish better economic ties between the two countries.

because the united states does not have good relations with cuba, canada's recent

decision may result in problems between washington and ottawa. in a recent interview,

peter sheffield, the canadian prime minister, indicated that his country was ready to

reestablish some sort of cooperation with cuba and that canada would do so as quickly

as possible. there is no doubt that this new development will be discussed at the opening

session of congress next tuesday.

Practice 5   *Read the following paragraph. Circle the capitalization errors and make corrections above.*

Paragraph 77

Crossing From Atlanta

EXAMPLE PARAGRAPH

It used to be difficult to travel directly from atlanta to europe, but this is certainly not the case nowadays. british airways offers several daily flights to london. Lufthansa, the national airline of germany, offers flights every day to frankfurt and twice a week to berlin. other european air carriers that offer direct flights from atlanta to europe are klm of the netherlands, sabena of belgium, and air france. however, the airline with the largest number of direct flights to any european city is not a european airline. delta airlines, which is the second largest airline in the united states, offers seventeen flights a day to twelve european cities, including paris, london, frankfurt, zurich, rome, and athens.

Appendix 3

Punctuation Practice

END PUNCTUATION

Three main kinds of punctuation occur at the end of an English sentence. You need to know how to use all three of them correctly.

1. **period (.)** A period is used at the end of a declarative sentence.

    This is a declarative sentence.

    This is not a question.

    All three of these sentences end with a period.

2. **question mark (?)** A question mark is used at the end of a question.

    Is this idea difficult?

    Is it hard to remember the name of this mark?

    How many questions are in this group?

3. **exclamation point (!)** An exclamation point is used at the end of an exclamation. It is less common than the other two marks.

    I can't believe you think this is difficult!

    This is the best writing book in the world!

    Now I understand all of these examples!

Practice 1   *Add the correct end punctuation.*

1. Congratulations I knew you would win the prize because you worked so hard

2. Do most people think that the governor was unaware of the theft

3. Do not open your test booklet until you are told to do so

4. Will the president attend the meeting

5. Jason put the dishes in the dishwasher and then watched TV

Practice 2   *Look at an article in any newspaper or magazine. Circle every end punctuation. Then answer these questions.*

1. How many final periods are there? _____ (or _____ %)

2. How many final question marks are there? _____ (or _____ %)

3. How many final exclamation points are there? _____ (or _____ %)

4. What is the total number of sentences? _____

Use this last number to calculate the percentages for each of the categories. Does the period occur most often?

COMMAS

The comma has several different functions in English. Here are some of the most common ones.

1. A comma separates a list of three or more things. There should be a comma between the items in a list.

> He speaks French and English.

> She speaks French, English, and Chinese.

2. A comma separates two sentences when there is a combining word such as *and, but, or,* and *so.*

> Six people took the course, but only five of them passed the test.

> Sammy bought the cake, and Paul paid for the ice cream.

> Students can register for classes in person, or they may submit their applications by mail.

3. A comma is used to separate an introductory word or phrase from the rest of the sentence.

> In conclusion, doctors are advising people to take more vitamins.

> First, you will need a pencil.

> Because of the heavy rains, many of the roads were flooded.

> Finally, add the nuts to the batter.

4. A comma is used to separate an appositive. An appositive is a word or group of words that renames a noun. An appositive provides additional information about the noun.

> <u>Washington</u>, *the first president of this country,* <u>was</u> a clever military leader.
>
>   SUBJECT (NOUN)   APPOSITIVE   VERB

In this sentence, the phrase *the first president of this country* is an appositive. This phrase renames or explains the noun *Washington.*

Practice 3   *Add commas as needed in these sentences. Some sentences may be correct,
and others may need more than one comma.*

1. For the past fifteen years Mary Parker has been both the director and producer of all the plays at this theater.

2. Despite all the problems we had on our vacation we managed to have a good time.

3. I believe the best countries to visit in Africa are Senegal Tunisia and Ghana.

4. She believes the best countries to visit in Africa are Senegal and Tunisia.

5. The third step in this process is to grate the carrots and the potatoes.

6. Third grate the carrots and the potatoes.

7. Blue green and red are strong colors. For this reason they are not appropriate for a living room wall.

8. Without anyone to teach foreign language classes next year the school will be unable to offer French Spanish or German.

9. The NEQ 7000 the very latest computer from Electron Technologies is not selling very well.

10. Because of injuries neither Carl nor Jamil two of the best players on the football team will be able to play in tomorrow's game.

APOSTROPHES

Apostrophes have two basic uses in English. They indicate either a contraction or a possession.

Contractions: Use an apostrophe in a contraction in place of the letter or letters that have been deleted.

he's (he is), they're (they are), I've (I have), we'd (we would)

Possession: Use an apostrophe to indicate possession. Add an apostrophe and the letter *s* after the word. If a plural word already ends in *s*, then just add the apostrophe.

Washington's term in office

Mrs. Popkes's three daughters

Yesterday's paper

The boy's books   (= one boy has some books)

The boys' books   (= several boys have one or more books)

Practice 4   *Correct the apostrophe errors in these sentences.*

1. Im going to Victors birthday party on Saturday.

2. The Smiths house is right next to the Wilsons house.

3. Hardly anyone remembers Roosevelts drastic action in the early part of this century.

4. It goes without saying that wed be better off without atomic weapons in this world.

5. The reasons that were given for the childrens bad behavior were unbelievable.

QUOTATION MARKS

These are three of the most common uses for quotation marks:

1. to mark the exact words that were spoken by someone

    "None of the solutions is correct," said the professor. (The comma is inside the quotation marks.)

    The king said, "I refuse to give up my throne." (The period is inside the quotation marks.)

    The king said that he refuses to give up his throne. (No quotation marks because the sentence does not include the king's exact words. This style is called indirect speech.)

2. to mark language that a writer has borrowed from another source

    The dictionary defines gossip as a "trivial rumor of a personal nature," but I would add that it is usually malicious.

    This research concludes that there was "no real reason to expect this computer software program to produce good results with high school students."

    According to an article in *Newsweek*, half of the money was stolen. (No quotes are necessary here because it is a summary of information rather than exact words from the article.)

3. to indicate when a word or phrase is being used in a special way

    The king believed himself to be leader of a democracy, so he allowed the prisoner to choose his method of dying. According to the king, allowing this kind of "democracy" showed that he was indeed a good ruler.

Practice 5   *Add quotation marks where necessary. Remember the rules for placing commas, periods, and question marks inside or outside the quotation marks.*

1. As I was leaving the room, I heard the teacher say, Be sure to study Chapter 7.

2. It is impossible to say that using dictionaries is useless. However, according to research published in the latest issue of the *General Language Journal*, 18.3% of students do not own a dictionary and 37.2% never use their dictionary. I find these statistics to be quite amazing.

3. My fiancée says that if I buy her a huge diamond ring, this would be a sure sign that I love her. I would like to know if there is a less expensive sign that would be acceptable to her.

4. When my English friend speaks of a "heat wave," I have to laugh because I come from Florida where we have sunshine most of the year. The days when we have to dress warmly are certainly few, and people wear shorts outside in almost every month of the year.

5. The directions on the package say, Open carefully. Add contents to 1 glass of warm water. Drink just before bedtime.

SEMICOLONS

The semicolon is used most often in compound sentences. Once you get used to using the semicolon, it will be a very easy and useful punctuation tool in your writing.

- Use a semicolon when you want to connect two simple sentences.
- The function of a semicolon is similar to that of a period. However, in order to use a semicolon, there must be a relationship between the sentences.

  Joey loves to play tennis. He's been playing since he was ten years old.
  Joey loves to play tennis; he's been playing since he was ten years old.

Both sentence pairs are correct. The main difference is that the semicolon in the second example signals the relationship between the ideas in the two sentences. Notice also that *he* is not capitalized in the second example.

Practice 6   *The following sentences use periods for separation. Rewrite the sentences. Replace the period with a semicolon and make any other change necessary.*

1. Gretchen and Bob have been friends since elementary school. They are also next door neighbors.

_____

2. The test was complicated. No one passed it.

_____

3. Tomatoes are necessary for a garden salad. Peas are not.

_____

4. Mexico lies to the south. Canada lies to the north.

_____

Practice 7   *Look at a copy of a newspaper or magazine. Circle all the semicolons on a page. The number should be relatively small.*

Note: If the topic of the article is technical or complex, there is a greater chance of finding semicolons. Semicolons are not usually used in informal or friendly writing. Thus, you might see a semicolon in an article on heart operations or educational research, but not in a letter or an ad for a household product.

EDITING FOR ERRORS

Practice 8   *Find the fourteen punctuation errors in this paragraph and make corrections.*

Paragraph 78

An Unexpected Storm

EXAMPLE PARAGRAPH

Severe weather is a constant possibility all over the globe; but we never really expect our own area to be affected However last night was different At about ten o'clock a tornado hit Lucedale This violent weather destroyed nine homes near the downtown area In addition to these nine houses that were completely destroyed many others in the area had heavy damage Amazingly no one was injured in last nights terrible storm Because

of the rapid reaction of state and local weather watchers most of the areas residents

saw the warnings that were broadcast on television

Practice 9   *Find the fifteen punctuation errors in this paragraph and make corrections.*

Paragraph 79

Deserts

Deserts are some of the most interesting places on earth A desert is not just a dry area

it is an area that receives less than ten inches of rainfall a year About one-fifth of the earth

is composed of deserts Although many people believe that deserts are nothing but hills of

sand this is not true In reality deserts have large rocks mountains canyons and even lakes For

instance only about ten percent of the Sahara Desert the largest desert on the earth is sand

Practice 10   *Find the fifteen punctuation errors in this paragraph and make corrections.*

Paragraph 80

A Review

I Wish I Could Have Seen His Face Marilyn Kings latest novel is perhaps her greatest

triumph In this book King tells the story of the Lamberts a poor family that struggles to survive

despite numerous hardships. The Lambert family consists of five strong personalities. Michael

Lambert has trouble keeping a job and Naomi earns very little as a maid at a hotel The three

children range in age from nine to sixteen. Dan Melinda and Zeke are still in school This

well-written novel allows us to step into the conflict that each of the children has to deal with.

Only a writer as talented as King could develop five independent characters in such an

outstanding manner The plot has many unexpected turns and the outcome of this story

will not disappoint readers While King has written several novels that won international praise

I Wish I Could Have Seen His Face is in many ways better than any of her previous works.

EXAMPLE PARAGRAPH

Appendix 4

Additional Grammar Practice

VERB TENSE

Practice 1   *Fill in the blanks with the correct form of the verb in parentheses.*

Paragraph 81

A Simple Recipe

Making tuna salad is not difficult. Put two cans of flaked tuna in a medium-sized bowl. With a fork, _____ (break) the fish apart. _____ (cut) up a large white onion or two small yellow onions. Add mayonnaise, salt, and pepper to taste. Be sure to include one-third cup of mayonnaise. Some people _____ (like) to have pieces of boiled eggs in the tuna salad.

Practice 2   *Fill in the blanks with the correct form of any appropriate verb.*

Paragraph 82

Who Killed Kennedy?

One of the most infamous moments in American history _____ in 1963. In that year, President John F. Kennedy _____ assassinated in Dallas, Texas. Since this event, there _____ many theories about what

PARAGRAPH

_____ on that fateful day. According to the official U.S. government report,

only one man _____ the bullets that _____ President

Kennedy. However, even today many people _____ that there

_____ several assassins.

Practice 3   *Fill in the blanks with the correct form of any appropriate verb.*

Paragraph 83

EXAMPLE PARAGRAPH

A Routine Routine

I have one of the most boring daily routines of anyone I _____ . Every

morning I _____ at 7:15. I _____ a shower and

_____ dressed. After that, I _____ breakfast and

_____ to the office. I _____ from 8:30 to 4:30. Then I

_____ home. This _____ five days a week without fail. Just for

once, I wish something different would happen!

Practice 4   *Fill in the blanks with the correct form of the verb in parentheses.*

Paragraph 84

EXAMPLE PARAGRAPH

The Shortest Term in the White House

William Henry Harrison (be) _____ the ninth president of the United States.

His presidency was extremely brief. In fact, Harrison (be) _____ president for

only one month. He (take) _____ office on March 4, 1841. Unfortunately, he

(catch) _____ a cold that (become) _____ pneumonia. On April

4, Harrison (die) _____ . He (become) _____ the first American

president to die while in office. Before becoming president, Harrison (study)

_____ to become a doctor and later (serve) _____ in the army.

Practice 5   *Fill in the blanks with the correct form of the verb in parentheses.*

Paragraph 85

The History of Bedford

One of the greatest tourist places in this area is Bedford. Bedford (be) _____ one of the oldest towns in this state. No one is certain when the first Europeans came to this area, but some families have been here for at least two hundred years. Because it is located at the foot of the Black Mountains near a lake, Bedford (attract) _____ a large number of settlers in the early colonial period. The mild climate also (draw) _____ settlers who (want) _____ to start farms in the area. For more than a hundred years after its initial settlement, not many new settlers (come) _____ to the area. However, now that tourists (discover) _____ this quaint little town, more and more people (move) _____ to Bedford once again.

ARTICLES

Practice 6   *Fill in the blanks with the correct article. If no article is required, write an* X.

Paragraph 86

_____ Simple Math Problem

There is _____ interesting mathematics brainteaser that always amazes _____ people when they first hear it. First, pick _____ number from _____ 1 to _____ 9. Subtract _____ 5. (You may have a negative number.) Multiply this answer by _____ 3. Now square _____ number. Then add _____ digits of _____ number. For _____ example, if your number is 81, add 8 and 1 to get an answer of _____ 9. If _____ number is less than _____ 5, add _____ 5. If _____ number is not less than _____ 5, subtract _____ 4. Now multiply this number by _____ 2. Finally, subtract _____ 6. If you have followed _____ steps correctly, _____ your answer is _____ 4.

Practice 7   *Fill in the blanks with the correct article. If no article is required, write an X.*

Paragraph 87

EXAMPLE PARAGRAPH

_____ Geography Problems among _____ American Students

Are _____ American high school students _____ less educated in _____ geography

than high school students in _____ other countries? According to _____ recent survey of

_____ high school students all over _____ globe, _____ U.S. students do not know

very much about _____ geography. For _____ example, _____ surprisingly large number

did not know _____ capital of _____ state in which they live. Many could not find _____

Mexico on a map even though Mexico is one of _____ two countries that _____ border

on _____ United States. Some _____ educators blame this lack of _____ geography

knowledge on the move away from memorization of material that has taken _____ place

in _____ recent years in American schools. Regardless of _____ cause, however, the

unfortunate fact appears to be that American _____ high school students are not learning

_____ enough about this subject _____ area.

Practice 8   *Fill in the blanks with the correct article. If no article is required, write an X.*

Paragraph 88

EXAMPLE PARAGRAPH

_____ Homeowners Can Save _____ Money with a New Free Service

People who are concerned that their monthly electricity bill is too high can now take

_____ advantage of _____ special free service offered by the local electricity company.

_____ company will do _____ home energy audit on any house to find out if _____

house is wasting _____ valuable energy. Homeowners can call _____ power company

to schedule _____ convenient time for _____ energy analyst to visit their home. The

audit takes only about _____ hour. _____ analyst will inspect _____ home and identify potential energy-saving _____ improvements. For _____ example, he or she will check

_____ thermostat, the air conditioning, and _____ seals around doors and windows. The

major energy use _____ problems will be identified, and _____ analyst will recommend

_____ ways to use _____ energy more efficiently.

Practice 9   *Fill in the blanks with the correct article. If no article is required, write an X.*

Paragraph 89

_____ Great Teacher

To this day, I am completely convinced that _____ main reason that I did so well in

my French class in _____ high school was the incredible teacher that I had, _____ Mrs.

de Montluzin. I had not studied _____ foreign language before I started _____ Mrs. de

Montluzin's French class. _____ idea of being able to communicate in a foreign language,

especially _____ French, intrigued me, but _____ idea also scared me. _____ French

seemed so difficult at first. We had so much _____ vocabulary to memorize, and we

had to do _____ exercises to improve our grammar. While it is true that there was _____

great deal of work to do, _____ Mrs. de Montluzin always tried her best to make French

class very interesting. She also gave us _____ suggestions for learning _____ French,

and these helped me a lot. Since this French class, I have studied a few other languages,

and my interest in _____ foreign languages today is due to _____ success I had in French

class with _____ Mrs. de Montluzin.

Practice 10   *Fill in the blanks with the correct article. If no article is required, write an X.*

Paragraph 90

_____ Surprising Statistics on _____ Higher Education in _____ United States

Although _____ United States is a leader in many areas, it is surprising that _____

number of Americans with _____ college degree is not as high as it is in some _____

other countries. Only about twenty-two percent of _____ Americans have attended

college for four or more years. To _____ most people, this rather low figure of one in

five is shocking. Slightly more than _____ sixty percent of _____ Americans between

_____ ages of twenty-five and forty have taken some _____ college classes. Though these

numbers are far from what _____ many people would expect in _____ United States,

these statistics are _____ huge improvement over figures at _____ turn of _____ century.

In _____ 1900, only about _____ 8 percent of all Americans even entered _____ college.

At _____ present time, there are about 16 million students attending _____ college.

EDITING FOR ERRORS

Practice 11   *This paragraph contains seven errors. They are in word choice (1), article (1), modal* (1), verb tense (2), and subject-verb agreement (2). Mark these errors and write the corrections.*

Paragraph 91

A Dangerous Driving Problem

Imagine that you are driving your car home from mall or the library. You come to a

bend in the road. You decide that you need to slow down a little, so you tap the brake

pedal. Much to your surprise, the car does not begin to slow down. You push the brake

pedal all the way down to the floor, but still anything happens. If your brakes will not

work, there are a few things that you can do. One was to pump the brakes. If this fails,

---

* Modals are *can, should, will, must, may,* and *might.* Modals appear before verbs. We do not use <u>to</u> between modals and verbs. *Incorrect:* I should to go with him. *Correct:* I should go with him. They do not have *-s* or *-ing* or *-ed.*

you should to try the emergency brake. If this also fail, you should try to shift the car into

a lower gear and rub the tires against the curb until the car come to a stop.

Practice 12   *This paragraph contains seven errors. They are in prepositions (2), articles (1), and verb tense (4). Mark these errors and write the corrections.*

Paragraph 92

The Start of My Love of Aquariums

My love of aquariums began a long time ago. Though I got my first fish when I am

just seven years old, I can still remember the store, the fish, and even salesclerk who waited

on me that day. It was 1965, and a dollar could buy a lot. I had made good grades on my

report card, and my uncle has rewarded me with a dollar. A few days later, I was finally

able to go to the local dime store for spend my money. I looked a lot of different things,

but I finally chose to buy a fish. We had an old fishbowl at home, so it seems logical with

me to get a fish. I must have spent fifteen minutes pacing back and forth in front of all the

aquariums before I finally chose my fish. It was a green swordtail, or rather, she was a green

swordtail. A few weeks later, she gave birth to twenty or thirty baby swordtails. Years

later, I can still remember this fish that gets me so interested in aquariums.

Practice 13   *This paragraph contains seven errors. They are in prepositions (2), articles (2), word forms (2), and subject-verb agreement (1). Mark these errors and write the corrections.*

Paragraph 93

The Modern Technology Endangers Drivers

One of the recent developments of modern technology, cellular phones, can be a

threat to safety. A recent study for Donald Redelmeier and Robert Tibshirani of the

University of Toronto showed that cellular phones do pose a risk to drivers. In fact, people

PARAGRAPH

who talk by the phone while driving are four times more likely to have an automobile

accident than those who do not use the phone while drive. The researchers studied 699

drivers who had been in an automobile accident while they were using their cellular

phones. The researchers concluded that the main reason for the accidents is not that

people used one hand for the telephone and only one for driving. Rather, the cause of

accidents was usually that the drivers became distracted, angry, or upset by the phone

call. The drivers then lost concentration and was more prone to a car accident.

Practice 14   *This paragraph contains seven errors. They are in passive voice (1), articles (2), word forms (3), and subject-verb agreement (1). Mark these errors and write the corrections.*

Paragraph 94

EXAMPLE PARAGRAPH

Problems with American Coins

Many foreigners who come to the United States have very hard time getting used to

America coins. The denominations of the coins are 1, 5, 10, 25, and 50 cents, and 1

dollar. However, only the first four commonly used in daily transactions. The smallest

coin in value is the penny, but it is not the smallest coin in size. The quarter is one-fourth

the value of a dollar, but it is not one-fourth as big as a dollar. There is a dollar coin, but

no one ever use it. In fact, perhaps the only place to find one is a bank. All of the coins

are silver-colored except for one, the penny. Finally, because value of each coin is not

clearly written on the coin as it is in many country, foreigners often experience problems

in monetarily transactions.

Practice 15   *This paragraph contains seven errors. They are in word order (1), articles (2), preposition (1), subject-verb agreement (1), and verb tense (2). Mark these errors and write the corrections.*

Paragraph 95

An Oasis of Silence

Life on this campus can be extremely hectic, so when I want the solitude, I go usually to the fourth floor of the library. The fourth floor has nothing but shelves and shelves of rare books and obscure periodicals. Because there are only a few small tables with some rather uncomfortable wooden chairs and no copy machines in this floor, few people are staying here very long. Students search for a book or periodical, found it, and then take it to a more sociable floor to photocopy the pages or simply browse through the articles. One of my best friends have told me that he does not like this floor that is so special to me. For him, it is a lonely place. For me, however, it is oasis of silence in a land of turmoil, a place where I can read, think, and write in peace.

Appendix 5

Peer Editing Sheets

PEER EDITING SHEET #1   **UNIT 1, Activity 15, p. 25**

Writer: _____ Date: _____

Peer editor: _____

1. What is the general topic of the paragraph? _____

2. What is the more specific topic? _____

   _____

3. If you can find the topic sentence, write it here. _____

   _____

4. How many sentences does the paragraph have? _____ Do all the sentences relate to the same

   topic? _____ If any sentence is not about the topic, write it here.

   _____

5. Can you understand the meaning of every sentence? _____

6. If you wrote "no" in number 5, write the unclear sentences here.

   _____

   _____

7. Does every sentence have a verb? If any sentence does not have a verb, write it here and add a verb.

   _____

8. Is the paragraph indented?   yes   no   (Circle one.)

   If it is not, circle the area where it should be indented.

9. Are any key nouns repeated? If so, comment on whether you think the repetition is effective.

   _____

   _____

10. If you have ideas or suggestions for making the paragraph better, write them here.

    _____

    _____

    _____

Writer: _____ Date: _____

Peer editor: _____

1. What is the general topic of the paragraph? _____

    _____

2. What is the specific topic? _____

    _____

3. Write the topic sentence here. _____

    _____

4. Is there any sentence that is not related to the topic? If so, write it here. _____

    _____

5. Does every sentence have a verb? If any sentence does not have a verb, write it here and add a verb.

    _____

    _____

6. Did you notice an error in subject-verb agreement? If so, write the sentence with the error here

    and make the correction. _____

    _____

7. Is there any sentence that is unclear to you? If so, write it here. _____

    _____

8. Is the paragraph indented?   yes   no   (Circle one.)

9. Do you have any suggestions for improving this paragraph? If so, write them here.

_____

_____

_____

PEER EDITING SHEET #3   **UNIT 3, Activity 11, p. 48**

Writer: _____ Date: _____

Peer editor: _____

1. What is the general topic of the paper?

   pets   food   conservation   computers   (Circle one.)

2. What is the specific topic? _____

   _____

3. Write the topic sentence here. _____

   _____

4. Do all the sentences relate to one topic? _____ If not, which sentence has extra material?

   _____

5. Is the paragraph indented?   yes   no   (Circle one.)

   _____

6. Punctuation: Does every sentence end with correct punctuation?   yes   no   (Circle one.)

7. Capitalization: Is the first word of every sentence capitalized?   yes   no   (Circle one.)

8. Are there any other capitalization errors?   yes   no   (If yes, mark them on the paper.)

9. If you answer "yes" to any of the following questions, circle the place on the paper.

   a. Does every sentence have a verb? _____

   b. Is there any problem with subject-verb agreement? _____

   c. Did you notice any comma splices? _____

   d. Are there any sentence fragments? _____

10. If you had trouble understanding any part of this paragraph, write the unclear part here.

_____

_____

_____

11. If you have any suggestions for improving this paragraph, write your comments here.

_____

_____

_____

Writer: _____ Date: _____

Peer editor: _____

1. What is the topic of the paragraph? _____

2. Write the topic sentence here. _____

   _____

3. Circle the controlling ideas in the topic sentence.

4. Do all the sentences in the paragraph add information about the controlling ideas? _____

   If you answered "no," describe any problems here. _____

   _____

   _____

5. Look at the pronouns. Do they each refer correctly to a noun? List any problems here.

   _____

   _____

6. Do all the sentences begin with a capital letter? _____ If you answered "no," where are the errors?

   _____

7. Check for comma splices and list the errors here.

   _____

   _____

8. If you found any sentence fragment errors, list them here:

_____

_____

9. Is the paragraph missing any important information? If so, write any questions that you think should be answered in this paragraph.

_____

_____

_____

10. Do you have any other suggestions for improving this paragraph?

_____

_____

_____

PEER EDITING SHEET #5   **UNIT 5, Activity 14, p. 77**

Writer: _____ Date: _____

Peer editor: _____

1. Check for these features:

   a. _____ Is there a topic sentence?

   b. _____ Do all the sentences relate to one topic?

   c. _____ Is the first line indented?

2. If you answered "no" to a. and b. in number 1, write comments here.

   Topic sentence: _____

   _____

   One topic: _____

   _____

3. What is the general topic of the paragraph? _____

4. Check for these errors. Circle them on the paper. Write the letters in parentheses above the circled word(s).

   sentence fragments (SF)   subject-verb agreement (S-V)

   comma splices (CS)   possessive pronoun reference (PR)

   capitalization (C)

5. Underline all the articles in the paragraph. Make sure each one is correct. Explain any corrections

   that are needed. _____

   _____

6. What is your overall impression of the paragraph?

_____

_____

7. Do you have any ideas or suggestions for improving the paragraph?

_____

_____

_____

Writer: _____ Date: _____

Peer editor: _____

1. What is the general topic of the paragraph? _____

2. Write the topic sentence here. _____

   _____

3. Is the topic sentence a definition?   yes   no   (Circle one.)

   Can you suggest any improvements for the topic sentence?

   _____

   _____

4. Is the paragraph indented?   yes   no   (Circle one.)

5. Does the writer use quotation marks? If so, are they used correctly?

6. Check for these errors. Circle any you find on the paper. Write the letters in parentheses above the circled word(s).

sentence fragments (SF)	subject-verb agreement (S-V)
comma splices (CS)	possessive pronoun reference (PR)
capitalization (C)	end punctuation (EP)
articles (A)	

7. Write one sentence from the paragraph that has an adjective clause. Is the clause correct?

   _____

   _____

8. Do you see any short, choppy sentences that could be combined for sentence variety? If so, write them and a suggested combination here. _____

_____

_____

9. Did you have any trouble understanding this paragraph?　　yes　　no　　(Circle one.)

If yes, tell where and why.

_____

_____

10. What questions do you have about the content? What other information should be in this paragraph?

_____

_____

_____

Writer: _____ Date: _____

Peer editor: _____

1. What process does this paragraph describe?

   _____

2. Write the topic sentence here. _____

   _____

3. How many steps does this process have? _____

4. Do you believe that the steps are in the correct order?   yes   no   (Circle one.)

   If you answered "no," what can the writer do to put the steps in the correct order?

   _____

   _____

5. What time or transition words or phrases does the writer use? Are they used correctly? (Review p.

   105 if you need help with these words.) _____

   _____

6. Is there a comma after all the introductory time words or phrases?   yes   no

   If not, mark the errors on the paper.

7. Does the writer include any technical terms? Do you understand what they mean, or do they need
   more explanation?

8. Check for these errors. Circle any you find on the paper. Write the letters in parentheses above the circled word(s).

sentence fragments (SF)	subject-verb agreement (S-V)
comma splices (CS)	possessive pronoun reference (PR)
capitalization (C)	end punctuation (EP)
articles (A)	adjective clauses (AJ)

9. What suggestions do you have for improving this paragraph?

_____

_____

_____

_____

Writer: _____ Date: _____

Peer editor: _____

1. What does this paragraph describe? _____

2. Write the topic sentence here. _____

   _____

3. Underline all the descriptive adjectives. How many are there? _____

4. Is every adjective placed correctly? If not, make corrections on the paper.

5. Read the adjectives again. Do you understand the connotation for each one? If you have questions about the precise meaning of any adjective, write your question here.

   _____

   _____

6. Check for these errors. Circle them on the paper. Write the letters in parentheses above the circled word(s).

sentence fragments (SF)	subject-verb agreement (S-V)
comma splices (CS)	possessive pronoun reference (PR)
capitalization (C)	end punctuation (EP)
articles (A)	adjective clauses (AJ)

7. Is the paragraph indented?   yes   no   (Circle one.)

8. Do you have a positive or a negative impression of the topic? What words gave you this impression?

   Positive: _____

   Negative: _____

9. Write any suggestions you have for improving the paragraph.

_____

_____

Writer: _____ Date: _____

Peer editor: _____

1. What is the general topic of this paragraph? _____

2. What is the writer's opinion about this topic? _____

   _____

3. Write the topic sentence here. _____

   _____

4. Check for correct word forms. Write any problems here. _____

   _____

   _____

5. Does the writer include an opposing opinion, or counterargument? If so, is this opinion refuted? Make notes about this on the paper.

6. Check for these errors. Circle any you find on the paper. Write the letters in parentheses above the circled word(s).

sentence fragments (SF)	subject-verb agreement (S-V)
comma splices (CS)	possessive pronoun reference (PR)
capitalization (C)	end punctuation (EP)
articles (A)	adjective clauses (AJ)
adjective placement (AP)	

7. Do the supporting sentences give enough facts to support the writer's opinion? Are there any supporting sentences that do not fit? Make any comments you want about the supporting facts.

_____

_____

_____

8. Read the concluding sentence. Does it restate the topic sentence or make a prediction? If not, make a revision suggestion for the writer.

_____

_____

_____

9. What other suggestions do you have for improving the paragraph?

_____

_____

_____

Writer: _____ Date: _____

Peer editor: _____

1. Write the topic sentence here. _____

   _____

2. Is this a narrative paragraph?   yes   no   (Circle one.)

3. Look for the beginning, middle, and end of the story. Summarize these parts here.

   Beginning: _____

   _____

   Middle: _____

   _____

   End: _____

   _____

4. Is there any part of the paragraph that is unclear to you? If so, write it here. What do you think

   the problem is? _____

   _____

   _____

5. Are the verb tenses consistent? If not, write any problems here. _____

   _____

   _____

6. Check for these errors. Circle any you find on the paper. Write the letters in parentheses above the circled word(s).

sentence fragments (SF)	subject-verb agreement (S-V)
comma splices (CS)	possessive pronoun reference (PR)
capitalization (C)	end punctuation (EP)
articles (A)	adjective clauses (AC)
adjective placement (AP)	word forms (WF)

7. Sometimes a narrative needs more information to sound complete or clear. Does this story need any more information? If so, what?

_____

_____

8. Write any other suggestions or comments you have about this paragraph.

_____

_____

_____

Writer: _____ Date: _____

Peer editor: _____

1. How many paragraphs are in the essay? _____ What is the topic of the essay?

   _____

2. Is there a thesis statement? _____ If yes, write it here. _____

   _____

   _____

3. Read paragraph 2. Does every supporting sentence connect to the first sentence

   of the paragraph (the topic sentence)? _____ If not, circle any sentence that

   doesn't fit.

4. Read paragraph 3. Write all the adjectives you find in the paragraph. _____

   _____

   _____

5. Find a sentence that contains a comma. Write the sentence here. _____

   _____

   _____

   In your opinion, is the comma used correctly? If it is not, correct the error on the

   paper.

6. Find the transition words in the essay and write them here. _____

_____

_____

In your opinion, are all the transition words used correctly? _____ If any are

not, suggest corrections on the paper.

Appendix 6

Answer Key

UNIT 1

Activity 1, p. 4: Answers will vary.

Writer's Note, pp. 5–6: *repetition:* 8; *subjects:* Braille, letters, people, Braille, character, dots, four, Braille, who, millions; 3; *present tense verbs:* is, have, read, uses, has, are (arranged), are (raised), are, gets, invented, are; *present tense:* invented; The action happened in the 1800s.

Activity 2, p. 6: Answers will vary.

Activity 3, pp. 6–7: **1.** To explain how to make egg salad sandwiches. **2–3.** Answers will vary.

Writer's Note, p. 8: 9; is, boil, peel, put, use, Add, Add, Mix, Allow, spread, enjoy; 5.

Activity 4, p. 8: Answers will vary.

Activity 5, p. 9: Answers will vary.

Writer's Note, p. 10: *number of sentences:* 11; *subjects:* time, I, I, I, I, it I, I, It, seats, It, this, we, hands, I, I, they I, I, I, plane, Time, I; *most common subject:* I; *verbs:* flew, was, remember, was, had wondered, would be like, boarded, flew, was, were, was, made, hit, turned, was, did not eat, gave, would not go, cannot tell, was, landed, erases, can remember; *number of verbs:* 23; *number of present tense verbs:* 4; *number of simple past verbs:* 16

Activity 6, p. 11: Answers will vary.

Activity 7, pp. 12–13: **1.** Reasons that parents allow or don't allow their kids to have a pet. **2.** 10; **3.** 1 (Cats are good pets, but I don't like it when they shed hair on the furniture.) **4.** <u>At some point, most parents have to decide whether to allow their children to have pets.</u> **5.** 8 [TBD]; **6.** Indentation. **7.** Yes. **8.** <u>Although many children want a pet, parents are divided on this issue for a variety of important reasons.</u> The information in both sentences is closely connected. The concluding sentence restates the main idea of the topic sentence.

Activity 8, p. 13: *Topic sentences:* Braille is a special system of writing and reading for blind people. An egg salad sandwich is one of the easiest and most delicious foods you can make. Although the first time I flew on a plane was many years ago, I can still remember how afraid I was that day. *Paragraph topics:* an explanation of Braille; how to make an egg salad sandwich; the story of a bad airplane flight ; *Are paragraphs indented?* yes; yes; yes

Activity 9, pp. 14–19:

Paragraph 6: **1.** Yes. William Henry Harrison, the ninth president of the United States, is famous for several things. **2.** significant information about William Henry Harrison **3.** Yes. **4.** Yes. **5.** It is ironic that William Henry Harrison, who was president for such a short time, is better known than many of the presidents who served full terms.

Paragraph 7: **1.** No. **2.** Why South Carolina is important **3.** Yes. **4.** No

Paragraph 8: **1.** Yes. Jim Thorpe won Olympic gold medals in 1912, but he wasn't allowed to keep them. **2.** U.S. Olympic Committee rules and their effect on Jim Thorpe **3.** Yes. **4.** Yes. **5.** Seventy years after, finally.

Paragraph 9: **1.** Yes. Statistics show that many Americans skip breakfast, and the reasons for this do not surprise me because I am a member of this group. **2.** Why I don't like to eat breakfast **3.** Yes **4.** Yes. **5.** No. The author has listed three strong supports for his opinion.

Paragraph 10: **1.** Yes. I can still remember the first day I taught a class. **2.** Memories of the first day of teaching **3.** No. I was wearing a new watch that day, too. **4.** No. **5.** I can still remember, first day.

Activity 10, pp. 19–20: **1.** This . . . state. **2.** More . . . residents. **3.** However . . . state? **4.** Some . . . problems. **5.** These Floridians . . . people. **6.** Some . . . Everglades. **7.** Others . . .water. **8.** Thus . . . thing.

Activity 11, p. 20: Titles will vary.

Activity 12, p. 22: **2.** C; <u>are talking</u>, <u>varies</u>; **3.** X; <u>stand</u>; **4.** C; <u>might touch</u>; **5.** C; <u>might be seen</u>; **6.** C; <u>stand</u>; **7.** X; <u>stands/is</u> <u>might see</u>; **8.** X; <u>varies</u>; **9.** X; <u>is</u>; **10.** C; <u>is</u>; <u>is</u>

Activity 13, p. 22: Titles will vary.

Activity 14, p. 23: Answers will vary.

Activity 15, p. 25: Answers will vary.

UNIT 2

Activity 1, p. 27: Answers will vary.

Activity 2, pp. 29–30: Answers will vary.

Activity 3, p. 31: Answers will vary.

Language Focus, pp. 32–33: **1.** live; **2.** is; **3.** carries; **4.** is

Activity 4, pp. 33–34: she <u>walks</u>, usually <u>arrives</u>, class <u>arrive</u>, class <u>begins</u>, She <u>has</u> to make sure that the teacher's aide. . . , . children <u>keep</u>, people <u>do</u>

Activity 5, p. 34: Answers will vary.

Activity 6, p. 34: Answers will vary.

UNIT 3

Activity 1, pp. 35–36: Answers may vary. Suggested answers: **1.** The best season for kids is winter. **2.** Soccer is the world's most popular sport. **3.** People from many different cultures live in Los Angeles. **4.** Many language students prefer bilingual dictionaries to monolingual dictionaries. **5.** French perfumes are expensive for a number of reasons. **6.** *An American Tragedy* is an excellent psychological novel.

Activity 2, pp. 38–39: Explanations may vary. Suggested explanations: **1.** SAT, two distinct sections, two different skills; *Explanation:* a listing of the two sections and skills in the SAT **2.** crash, jumbo jet, baffled investigators; *Explanation:* what has puzzled investigators **3.** Buying a house, renting an apartment, advantages; *Explanation:* why renting an apartment is better than buying a house **4.** Research, dark green, leafy vegetables, reduce, cancer; *Explanation:* medical benefits or decreased risk of cancer from eating these vegetables **5.** Crossword puzzles, educational, fun, addictive; *Explanation:* reasons people do crossword puzzles

Activity 3, pp. 39–40: Explanations will vary. **1.** Research has shown that girls are better at languages than boys. **2.** Cats are better pets than dogs for many reasons. **3.** Yesterday was the worst day of my life. **4.** Because of his numerous contributions to the United States, George Washington is often called the Father of Our Country. **5.** The current population of Canada is a reflection of the international background of its citizens and immigrants.

Activity 4, pp. 40–41: Answers will vary.

Activity 5, pp. 41–43: Answers will vary. Possible topic sentences: **1.** People like sports cars for different reasons. **2.** Dinosaurs differ from modern reptiles in two ways. **3.** Exercise can benefit people in several important ways. **4.** Popcorn is a simple but excellent snack food. **5.** An amazing new method for learning foreign language vocabulary has two stages.

Activity 6, pp. 43–44: **1.** Correct **2.** Correct **3.** extent, **4.** Correct **5.** growing, **6.** tourists, **7.** However, **8.** Correct **9.** Muslim, **10.** king, **11.** colony, **12.** Thus,

Activity 7, p. 44: Titles will vary.

Activity 8, pp. 46–47: **2.** SF; Most of the flights were canceled due to the torrential rains and high winds. **3.** CS; Computer programs can help students learn a foreign language. Many students use the language programs in the computer center. **4.** Correct **5.** CS; *Family* is a locally produced magazine, and the quality of the writing is very high. *or:* *Family* is a locally produced magazine. The quality of the writing is very high. **6.** SF; Last year the magazine won several awards for the content and the style of its stories.

Activity 9, p. 48: Answers will vary.

Activity 10, p. 48: Answers will vary.

Activity 11, p. 48: Answers will vary.

UNIT 4

Activity 1, p. 50: Predictions may vary. **1.** *controlling ideas*: best cities on the east coast, Washington D.C.; *prediction*: reasons and examples showing why Washington, D.C., is a good place to visit **2.** *controlling ideas*: interesting career, flight attendant; prediction: interesting aspects of being a flight attendant **3.** *controlling ideas*: respect and admire, grandmother Carla; *prediction*: good qualities of my grandmother

Activity 2, pp. 51–52: No written answers.

Activity 3, pp. 52–53: **a.** TS 2 **b.** TS 1 **c.** TS 1 **d.** TS 2 **e.** TS 1 **f.** TS 1 **g.** TS 2 **h.** TS 1

Activity 4, pp. 53–54: Answers may vary. Suggested answers: **1.** What are the four kinds of snakes? **2.** What are the adverse effects? **3.** How will computers eliminate libraries? **4.** Why isn't learning to play the piano difficult? **5.** What happened when your boyfriend broke up with you?

Activity 5, pp. 54–55: Answers will vary.

Activity 6, p. 56: Answers will vary.

Activity 7, pp. 57–59: *Paragraph 24:* **1.** good supporting sentence: It tells a reason for using chlorine, which is mentioned in the previous sentence. **2.** unrelated sentence: No connection between accidental poisoning and maintaining your pool. **3.** good supporting sentence: Another step in maintaining a swimming pool. *Paragraph 25:* **1.** good supporting sentence: First example of how to relax. **2.** good supporting sentence: Another example of how to relax. **3.** unrelated sentence: New information not related to the topic of how to relax and fall asleep.

Activity 8, p. 60: **1.** It **2.** they **3.** it **4.** We **5.** It

Activity 9, pp. 62–64: *Paragraph 26:* TS: <u>When I first started going to college, I was surprised at all the studying I had to do</u>. Unrelated sentences: none. Concluding sentence: <u>Although I was surprised at first at the amount of work I had to do, I managed to change my habits and become a good university student</u>. *Paragraph 27* TS: <u>Caring for river turtles is easier than many people think</u>. Unrelated sentences: If you have a large turtle, you will need to construct a small pond in your back yard. Concluding sentence: <u>After you have finished these simple steps, your home is ready for your new pet</u>. *Paragraph 28:* TS: <u>There are four easy ways to prepare a delicious and nutritious egg</u>. Unrelated sentences: Some people believe that brown eggs taste better than white eggs. Concluding sentence: none; answers will vary. (*Hint:* Restate the main idea, summarize the ideas, or make a prediction.)

Activity 10, p. 64: Answers will vary.

Activity 11, p. 64: Answers will vary.

UNIT 5

Activity 1, pp. 66–67: Answers will vary. Sample answers: **1.** There are three important steps to follow if you want to enter a university. **2.** The Capilano Bridge is not an ordinary bridge. **3.** I'll never forget my first rock concert.

Activity 2, pp. 67–68: Indent the first line. **C**anada and the United **S**tates   **T**he game ice,   around**.**   puck   goalie**.**   goal**.**

Activity 3, p. 68: Titles will vary.

Activity 4, pp. 68–69: Georgia**,**   **A**labama**,**   Carolina   beverage**.**   **O**nce   **S**tir   **A**fter that**,**   minutes**.**

Activity 5, p. 69: Titles will vary.

Activity 6, p. 70: **a.** 2, supporting   **b.** 5, concluding   **c.** 1, topic   **d.** 3, supporting   **e.** 4, supporting

Activity 7, pp. 70–71: Titles will vary.

Activity 8, p. 71: **1.** Shipbuilding traditions. **2.** The art of shipbuilding has some odd traditions, and one of the most interesting of all has its roots in Greek and Roman history. **3.** To explain why shipbuilders used coins. **4.** Answers will vary.

Activity 9, pp. 72–73: *Paragraph 35.* England and India do not have any land in the Arctic. *Paragraph 36.* It snows a lot in the Arctic.

Activity 10, p. 73: First,   moon rocks,   space crafts,   Next,   After that,   Finally,

Activity 11, p. 74: *Answers to student questions:* Should I capitalize *lake?* Yes. Should I put a period or a comma after *rains?* Period. Do I need a comma after *unfortunately?* Yes. Do I need to put commas in this list of rivers? Yes—and after *Everglades?* Yes. Is the verb *prevents* okay with this subject? No, use *prevent. Error correction:* unique,   **F**lorida   environment**.**   **L**ake Okeechobee**.**   **A**fter heavy rains,   **U**nfortunately,   **F**or example,   **L**ittle,   prevent~~s~~   **W**ithout   **E**verglades

Activity 12, p. 76: **The** Best   is **the** best   ~~a~~ spaghetti   ~~the~~ fried fish   ~~the~~ beans   **a** cooking contest   ~~the~~ southern Louisiana   ~~the~~ seafood   ~~the~~ red beans   ~~the~~ gumbo   **a** cookbook

Activity 13, p. 77: Answers will vary.

Activity 14, p. 77: Answers will vary.

Activity 15, p. 77: Answers will vary.

UNIT 6

Activity 1, pp. 81–86: *Paragraph 40:* **1.** The dictionary definition of gumbo does not make it sound as delicious as it really is. **2–5.** Answers will vary. *Paragraph 41:* **1.** According to *The American Heritage Dictionary*, gossip is a "trivial rumor of a personal nature," but this definition makes gossip sound harmless. **2.** Gossip is worse than the definition indicates. The writer mentions this in several places: *damage; can't do anything to answer or protect himself or herself; hurt feelings; lost career; gossip is much worse.* **3.** Yes **4–5.** Answers will vary. *Paragraph 42:* **1.** A pretzel is a salted, glazed biscuit that is often shaped or twisted like a knot. **2.** It is not a dictionary definition. **3–5.** Answers will vary.

Activity 2, p. 87: **2.** "a short . . . purpose," **3.** "a narcotic . . . addictive," **4.** "extremely . . . rich," **5.** "parents . . . children," **7.** announced, "Beginning . . . covering." **8.** asked, "Where . . . go?" **9.** opponent, "Are . . . out?" **10.** "I . . . longer,"

Activity 3, p. 88: **a.** 5 **b.** 4 **c.** 1 **d.** 7 **e.** 3 **f.** 2 **g.** 6

Activity 4, pp. 88–89: Titles will vary.

Activity 5, pp. 89–90: **1.** Learning vocabulary **2.** The key-word method, which can help foreign language learners remember new vocabulary, is gaining popularity among teachers and students. **3.** To explain a new method for learning vocabulary. **4.** Two; the Japanese example and the Malay example. **5.** It would be difficult to understand the topic because readers are unlikely to have any background knowledge about this topic. **6.** Answers will vary.

Activity 6, p. 92: *that* <u>features high winds and heavy rains</u>; noun: *storm*; *that* <u>can flood a whole town</u>; noun: *surge*; *which* <u>have the most hurricanes</u>; noun: *months*; *who* <u>live in a given area</u>; noun: *residents*; *that* <u>surprised the residents of Galveston, Texas, in 1900</u>; noun: *hurricane*; *that* <u>exist</u>; noun: *phenomena*

Activity 7, pp. 93–94: Answers will vary.

Activity 8, pp. 96–97: *Paragraph 45:* We can see patience in a person who is waiting at a street corner although it is starting to drizzle. *Paragraph 46:* Alaska is not a cold, barren place all the time, and it was not a waste of money. *Paragraph 47:* In ancient times, people used clay pottery for plates and bowls.

Activity 9, p. 98: Answers will vary.

Activity 10, p. 98: Answers will vary.

Activity 11, p. 98: Answers will vary.

UNIT 7

Activity 1, pp. 100–104: *Paragraph 48:* **1.** Eating a juicy taco is not easy—it requires following specific directions. **2.** b. Do you want to eat it alone or with other people? c. Decide on the steps to follow. **3.** Answers may vary. *Paragraph 49:* **1.** Although the process for applying to an American university is not complicated, it is important to follow each step. **2.** Start the application process early. **3.** No. It is not the topic of this paragraph. **4.** 8; number 2: get information; write for information or use the Internet. *Paragraph 50:* **1.** b. Pour three cups of water into the pot. c. Heat the water until it boils. d. Remove the water from the heat. e. Add coffee and sugar. **2.** Gently stir the mixture and return it to the heat until you can see foam on top. **3.** Pour three small cups of water into the pot and heat it until it boils. *Or:* Pour three small cups of water into the pot and then heat it until it boils. **4.** Answers may vary. *Sample answer:* a. You need a special pot. b. It takes a long time to make this coffee. c. You have to pay careful attention to every step of the process.

Language Focus, p. 105: **2.** The first step; Next; After; Then; In addition; Finally; In addition to these steps

Activity 2, p. 106: **a.** 5 (no time phrase) **b.** 6, after **c.** 4, just before **d.** 2, first **e.** 3, at the same time **f.** 7, after **g.** 1, following **h.** 8, preceding

Activity 3, pp. 106–107: Titles will vary.

Activity 4, pp. 107–108: **1.** How to serve in tennis **2.** Many people think serving in tennis is difficult, but the following steps show that it is quite easy. **3.** Serving is not difficult. **4.** It's a supporting sentence (for one of the steps).

Activity 5, pp. 108–109: **a.** 3, First, **b.** 9, One week later, **c.** 10 **d.** 4, this, **e.** 8 **f.** 5, temperature, **g.** 1 **h.** 2 **i.** 6 **j.** 7, After that,

Activity 6, p. 109: Titles will vary.

Activity 7, pp. 110–111: Some answers may vary. **1.** This hot, thick coffee is difficult to make. **2.** A *jezve* is a coffeepot that has a handle but doesn't have a lid. **3.** Jenny has a very painful sunburn because she fell asleep at the beach. **4.** The sleepy children watched a funny cartoon on Saturday morning TV. **5.** To eat a taco, you must turn your head slowly at a twenty-degree angle.

Activity 8, p. 111: Original writing will vary.

Activity 9, p. 111: Peer editing will vary.

Activity 10, p. 111: Writing will vary.

UNIT 8

Activity 1, p. 113: Answers will vary.

Activity 2, p. 114: Answers will vary.

Activity 3, pp. 114–118: *Paragraph 54:* **1.** A subway station. **2.** Answers may vary. **3.** *Sight:* broken clock showing 4:30; poster; deep, blue skies; lone palm tree; sapphire waters; *smell:* smelly staircase; *hearing:* crying child; two old men are arguing; little noise **4.** Present progressive tense (to make the reader feel like he or she is experiencing the description). *Paragraph 55:* **1.** A tornado. **2.** Past tense. Suggested answers: begin, touch, hurl, rip, roar, be, can. **3.** *Sight:* began to descend; swirling clouds; ripped the roof from an old house; *hearing:* winds roared like a wild beast. **4.** Suggested adjectives: long, slender, swirling, deadly, old, ferocious, wild, delicate (Feeling descriptions will vary.) *Paragraph 56:* **1.** What Mother did for her rose garden. **2.** Answers may vary, but we think that all of the sentences are necessary. **3.** a. She ripped out weeds that might be a danger to the flowers. b. She killed insects.

Activity 4, pp. 120–121: **1.** C **2.** on the *old* blackboard **3.** a *long* letter **4.** C **5.** a *great* place **6.** C **7.** C **8.** C **9.** an *excellent* example **10.** *deep green* feathers

Activity 5, pp. 121–122: Answers will vary.

Activity 6, p. 123: Answers will vary.

Activity 7, p. 124: **1.** *Paragraph 57:* the vital quality of the Blue River; *Paragraph 58:* the polluted quality of the Blue River **2.** The Blue River is attractive and full of life (important, fresh, clear, wide, colorful, abundant, beautiful, tall, shade, green, healthy, wild, sweet, grassy) **3.** The Blue River is unappealing and polluted (sluggish, brown, few, scrawny, limited, dirty, old, gray, dying, wild, polluted) **4.** abundant/limited, green/gray, healthy/dying, sweet/polluted

Activity 8, pp. 125–126: Answers will vary.

Activity 9, p. 126: Answers will vary.

Activity 10, p. 127: Answers will vary.

Activity 11, p. 127: Answers will vary.

UNIT 9

Activity 1, pp. 129–132: *Paragraph 60:* **1.** Studies show that there has been an increase in the number of people who support "medicide," which happens when people with terminal diseases choose to end their lives rather than continue living. **2.** Answers will vary. **3.** a. People cannot live with pain. b. They have financial problems. c. They lose hope. **4.** Many people believe that medicide is an "unnatural way to die" and should remain illegal. **5.** The author is in favor of medicide. **6.** Answers will vary. *Paragraph 61:* **1.** No matter how much money Pepsi spends on advertising, Coke will always be better in my opinion. **2.** in my opinion; I think; for me **3–4.** Answers will vary. *Paragraph 62:* **1.** The author thinks mandatory school uniforms are a good thing. **2.** Everyone will be equal. Getting ready for school will be easier. Students will perform better at school. **3.** School uniforms take away personal freedom.

Activity 2, p. 133: *Good topic sentences:* 2, 4, 5, and 8.

Activity 3, p. 134: *Fact:* **1.** Studies show that there has been an increase in the number of people who support "medicide." **2.** Staying in the hospital for a long time often causes a financial burden on the family. *Opinion:* **1.** People should not be forced to continue living if they are in severe pain. **2.** Sick people should certainly have the right to end their lives if they want.

Language Focus, pp. 134–136:

Noun	Verb	Adjective	Adverb
finance	finance	financial	financially
illness		ill	
illegality		illegal	illegally
desire	desire	desirable	desirably
sweetness	sweeten	sweet	sweetly
simplicity	simplify	simple	simply
equality	equalize	equal	equally
benefit	benefit	beneficial	beneficially
freedom	free	free	freely

Activity 4, p. 137: **1.** X, believe **2.** C **3.** X, beneficial **4.** X, freely **5.** C **6.** X, simple **7.** X, sweet **8.** X, logic **9.** X, increase **10.** C

Activity 5, pp. 137–138: **a.** 5, F **b.** 2, F **c.** 4, F **d.** 6, O **e.** 1, O **f.** 3, F

Activity 6, pp. 138–139: Titles will vary.

Activity 7, p. 140: Answers will vary.

Activity 8, p. 140: Answers will vary.

Activity 9, p. 140: Answers will vary.

UNIT 10

Activity 1, pp. 143–147: *Paragraph 65:* **1.** I'll never forget the first time I got lost in New York City. **2.** Macy's department store. **3.** Probably under ten. **4.** a **5.** b **6.** a **7.** To tell a story about a time that he was afraid. *Paragraph 66:* **1.** My most embarrassing moment happened when I was working in a Mexican restaurant. **2.** She lost her skirt in front of the restaurant customers. **3.** b **4.** a **5.** a **6.** To tell an embarrassing but funny story. *Paragraph 67:* **1.** Making new friends. **2.** I learned the hard way how to make friends in a new school. **3.** At my old school in New Jersey, I was on the football and track team, so I was very popular and had lots of friends. Then, when I was sixteen years old, my parents decided to move to Florida. **4.** Going to a new school was not easy for me. The first few days in my new school were extremely hard. All the students dressed casually in shorts and T-shirts instead of a school uniform. Some kids tried to be nice to me, but I didn't want to talk to them. They looked and acted funny! After a few weeks, I realized that no one even tried to talk to me anymore. I began to feel lonely **5.** Two months passed before I swallowed my pride and got the courage to talk to a few classmates. Finally, I realized that they were normal people, just like me. I began to develop some relationships. I learned a valuable lesson about making friends that year. **6.** Answers will vary.

Activity 2, p. 148: My Best Friend Luke; The Day I Almost Died; A Wonderful Day in the Mountains

Activity 3, pp. 148–149: **a.** 4 **b.** 6 **c.** 2 **d.** 1 **e.** 3 **f.** 7 **g.** 5

Activity 4, pp. 149–150: Titles will vary.

Background: My trip to Mexico City in September 1985 was not my first time there, but this unforgettable trip helped me realize something about life.

Beginning: I flew to Mexico City on September 17. The seventeenth and eighteenth were uneventful days. I visited a few friends and did a little sightseeing. On the evening of the eighteenth, I had a late dinner with some friends that I had not seen in several years. It was a very peaceful evening.

Middle: At 7:18 the next morning, a severe earthquake measuring 8.1 on the Richter scale hit Mexico City. I was asleep, but the violent movement of my bed from side to side woke me up. Then I could hear the rumble of the building as it was shaking. When I looked at my room, I could see that the floor moving up and down like water in the ocean. Because the doorway is often the strongest part of a house, I tried to stand up in the doorway of the bedroom, but I could not even stand up. As I tried to stand up, I could hear the stucco walls of the building cracking. I was on the third floor of a six-story building, and I thought the building was going to collapse. I really believed that I was going to die

End: In the end, approximately 50,000 people died in this terrible tragedy, but I was lucky enough not to be among them. This unexpected disaster taught me that life can be over at any minute, so it is extremely important for us to live every day as if it is our last. Life is too short.

Language Focus, pp. 150–151: jumped, rode, looked, wondered, arrived, saw, waited, gave, frightened, reminded, was working, hoped, was, looked up, was calling, stepped up, gave, glanced, knew, heard, was, turned, heard, is, couldn't believe, happened. took, left, would write

Activity 5, p. 152: was, got, tried and tried, get, was, was eating, began, was sitting, asked, could read, said, started, began, was, was looking, told, was, studied, gave, was, was

Activity 6, pp. 153–156: *Paragraph 71: 1. Paragraph 72: 4. Paragraph 73: 5. Paragraph 74: 2. Paragraph 75: 3.*

Activity 7, p. 156: Answers will vary.

Activity 8, p. 156: Answers will vary.

Activity 9, p. 157: Answers will vary.

UNIT 11

Activity 1, p. 159: Answers will vary.

Activity 2, p. 161: 1. a. E, b. P. 2. a. P, b. E. 3. a. P, b. E. 4. a. E, b. P. 5. a. E, b. P.

Activity 3, p. 166: Answers will vary. Possible answers include: (computer literacy) I. Introduction. II. Body (paragraph 2): It is needed in academic situations. III. Body (paragraph 3): It is needed in the workforce. IV. Body (paragraph 4): What schools are doing about this growing need. V. Conclusion (paragraph 6). (grandmother Josephine) I. Introduction. II. Body (paragraph 2): She taught me to be strong. III. Body (paragraph 3): She taught me to be kind. IV. Body (paragraph 4): She gave me unconditional love. V. Conclusion (paragraph 6).

Activity 4, p. 167: Answers will vary.

Activity 5, p. 167: 1. a story. 2. opinion. 3. paragraph 3. 4. paragraph 4. 5. paragraph 5.

Activity 6, p. 169: I. B. There are many benefits to being bilingual. II. A. One of the most basic advantages of being bilingual is a linguistic one. II. B. 3. Putting your 'John Hancock' on something is a phrase that includes historical reference. II C. Finally, widespread bilingualism can contribute to global awareness. II. C. 2. Bilingualism can increase sympathy among nations. III. B. People who 'lose' a language are making a grave mistake.

Activity 7, p. 171: Answers will vary. Some possible answers are: there are more cultural activities; there is more opportunity for professional development; you can remain anonymous if you want.

Activity 8, p. 172: Answers will vary.

Activity 9, p. 173: Answers will vary.

Activity 10, p. 174: Answers will vary.

APPENDIX 1

No questions.

APPENDIX 2

Practice 1, p. 170: **1.** The, Miami **2.** Does, Jill, West Bay Apartments **3.** The, New York, Saturday, Sunday **4.** sister, Rachel, Rosalyn **5.** If, Mercedes, I, I'd

Practice 2, p. 170: **1.** States, America **2.** July **3.** Paris **4.** Levi's (Answers will vary.) **5.** John, Jacqueline **6.** World War II **7.** McDonald's **8.** China **9.** December, January, February **10.** Answers will vary.

Practice 3, p. 171: **1.** My Favorite Food **2.** Living in Miami **3.** The Best Restaurant in Town **4.** Mr. Smith's New Car **5.** A New Trend in Hollywood **6.** Why I Left California **7.** My Side of the Mountain **8.** No More Room for a Friend

Practice 4, p. 171: According, *Newsweek,* (optional: Prime Minister), Because, Canada, Cuba, United States, Cuba, Canada's, Washington, Ottawa, In, Peter Sheffield, Canadian, (optional: Prime Minister) Cuba, Canada, There, Congress, Tuesday

Practice 5, p. 172: Atlanta, Europe, British Airways, London, Germany, Frankfurt, Berlin, Other, European, Atlanta, Europe, KLM, Netherlands, Sabena, Belgium, Air France, However, European, European, Delta Airlines, United States, European, Paris, London, Frankfurt, Zurich, Rome, Athens

APPENDIX 3

Practice 1, p. 173: **1.** Congratulations! hard. **2.** theft? **3.** so. **4.** meeting? **5.** TV.

Practice 2, p. 174: Answers will vary.

Practice 3, p. 175: **1.** years, **2.** vacation, **3.** Senegal, Tunisia, **4.** (no commas) **5.** (no commas) **6.** Third, **7.** Blue, green, For this reason, **8.** year, French, Spanish, **9.** The NEQ 7000, Electron Technologies, **10.** injuries, Jamil, team,

Practice 4, p. 176: **1.** I'm, Victor's **2.** The Smiths', Wilsons' **3.** Roosevelt's **4.** we'd **5.** children's

Practice 5, p. 177: **1.** "Be sure to study Chapter 7." **2.** (no quotation marks) **3.** (no quotation marks) **4.** "summer," **5.** "Open carefully. Add contents to 1 glass of warm water. Drink just before bedtime."

Practice 6, p. 178: **1.** Gretchen and Bob have been friends since elementary school; they are also next door neighbors. **2.** The test was complicated; no one passed it. **3.** Tomatoes are necessary for a garden salad; peas are not. **4.** Mexico lies to the south; Canada lies to the north.

Practice 7, p. 178: Answers will vary.

Practice 8, pp. 178–179: globe, affected. However, different. Lucedale. downtown area. destroyed, damage. Amazingly, night's storm. watchers, area's television.

Practice 9, p. 179: earth. area; year. deserts. sand, true. reality, rocks, mountains, canyons, lakes. instance, Sahara Desert, earth, sand.

Practice 10, p. 179: *Face,* King's novel, triumph. book, Lamberts, job, hotel. Dan, Melinda, school. manner. turns, readers. praise,

APPENDIX 4

Practice 1, p. 180: break, cut, like

Practice 2, pp. 180–181: *sample answers:* was, was, have been, happened, shot, killed, believe, were

Practice 3, p. 181: *sample answers:* know, wake up, take, get, eat, go, work, go, happens

Practice 4, p. 181: was, was, took, caught, became, died, became, studied, served

Practice 5, p. 182: (Some answers may vary) is, attracted, drew, wanted, came, are discovering, are moving

Practice 6, p. 182: (Articles listed consecutively in context; all other choices are X.) A Simple, an interesting, pick a number, square the number, the digits of the number, If the number, If the number is not, the steps

Practice 7, p. 183: (Articles listed consecutively in context; all other choices are X.) a recent survey, the globe, a surprisingly, the capital of the state, the two countries, the United States, the cause

Practice 8, pp. 183–184: (Articles listed consecutively in context; all other choices are X.) a special, The company, a home energy, the house is wasting, the power company, a convenient, an energy analyst, an hour, The analyst, the home and identify, the thermostat, the seals, the analyst will

Practice 9, p. 184: (Articles listed consecutively in context; all other choices are X.) A Great Teacher, the main reason, a foreign, The idea, the idea also, a great deal, the success

Practice 10, pp. 184–185: (Articles listed consecutively in context; all other choices are X.) The Surprising, the United States, the United States, the number of Americans, a college degree, the ages of, the United States, a huge, the turn of the century, the present

Practice 11, pp. 185–186: **the** mall, **nothing** happens, brakes **do** not, One **is,** should **try,** also **fails,** car **comes** to a stop

Practice 12, p. 186: when I **was** just seven, remember the store, the fish, and even **the** salesclerk, uncle **had** rewarded, store **to** spend, looked **at, seemed** logical **to/for** me, **got** me so interested

Practice 13, p. 186–187: ~~The~~ Modern Technology, **by** Donald Redelmeier, talk **on** the phone, while **driving,** accident **was** not, cause of **the** accidents, **were** more prone

Practice 14, p. 187: **a** very hard, getting used to **American** coins, first four **are** commonly used, no one ever **uses,** because **the** value, many **countries,** in **monetary**

Practice 15, p. 188: ~~the~~ solitude, I **usually go,** copy machines **on,** people **stay, find** it, best friends **has** told, it is **an** oasis

APPENDIX 5

Peer editing sheets: Answers will vary.